Entrepreneur **POCKET GUIDES**

Start Your
REAL ESTATE
Career

Entrepreneur Press and
Rich Mintzer

Ep
Entrepreneur®
Press

Editorial Director: Jere L. Calmes
Advisory Editor: Jack Savage
Cover Design: Beth Hansen-Winter
Production and Composition: Eliot House Productions

This publication is designed to provide accurate and authoritative information in regard to the subject matter covered. It is sold with the understanding that the publisher is not engaged in rendering legal, accounting or other professional services. If legal advice or other expert assistance is required, the services of a competent professional person should be sought.

Library of Congress Cataloging-in-Publication Data
    Mintzer, Richard.
      Start your real estate career/by Rich Mintzer.
        p.   cm.
      ISBN-13: 978-1-59918-001-4 (alk. paper)
      ISBN-10: 1-59918-001-4 (alk. paper)
       1. Real estate agents. 2. Real estate business. I. Title.
    HD1375.M484 2006
    333.33023'73—dc22   2005030199

Printed in Canada
12 11 10 09 08 07 06   10 9 8 7 6 5 4 3 2 1

Start Your
REAL
ESTATE
Career

Other Entrepreneur Pocket Guides include

Start Your Restaurant Career

Contents

Acknowledgments. xi

Preface xiii

Chapter 1

All About Real Estate 1

Profile: Susan Berman. 1

History 5

Profile: RE/MAX. 12

The Real Estate Market 14

The Industry Today 15

Chapter 2

Is Real Estate the Right Career for You?. 19

Profile: John Galletta 19

How Do You Like to Spend Your Day? 23

Are You a People Person?. 24

Is Research Your Thing? 25

Can You Sell? 26

How Do You Feel about Flexible Hours? 29

Are You Proactive? 30

What Skills and Abilities Do You Need?. 31

Do You Have the "Real Estate" Personality? 33

Chapter 3

Training, Education, and Background 37

Profile: James Taylor Lott. 37

Real Estate Courses: What to Expect 39

Your Licensing Exam 40

Ongoing Training 43

Finding the Right Real Estate Firm for You. 43

Spending Money to Make Money 48

On-the-Job Training. 50

Additional Training and Special Skills to
    Enhance Your Career 51

Chapter 4

Beyond an Agent:
Other Real Estate Career Options 59

Profile: Jo Falcone. 59

Real Estate Broker 61

Commercial Agents and Brokers 62

Real Estate Office Manager 65

Property Manager 66
Land Broker and Developer. 68
Real Estate Appraiser 68
Urban Planner 70
Mortgage Broker 72
Researcher 73
Salaries 74

Chapter 5
What You Need to Know 77

Profile: Sandra Lippman 77
Selling Homes, Not Just Houses 79
Selling Businesses, Not Just Office or Retail Space 86
Know Your Neighborhood 88
Appraisals 89
Deeds, Titles, Permits, and other Documents 90
Real Estate Taxes 91
Down Payments and Mortgages 92
Closing Costs 95
The Future of Your Real Estate Market 96
Commissions. 97
A Walk-Through of the Process of Selling a Property. . . . 98

Chapter 6
The Work Environment and
Your Responsibilities. 101

Profile: Nancy Ferri 101

Setting Up Your Office 103

Generating Leads 106

Floor Duty 111

Are You a Team Player? 111

Handling the Competition 112

Fiduciary Responsibility 114

Errors and Omissions (E&O) Insurance 115

Discrimination and Fair Housing Laws 115

Multiple Listing Service 116

Disclosures and Waivers 116

Virtual Tours. 117

The Industry Open House 118

The Public Open House 118

Research 120

Chapter 7
Try Before You Buy 123

Profile: David Fischer 123

Internships and Part-Time Jobs. 125

Mentors and Learning from Professionals 129

Professional Wisdom. 134

Chapter 8
Getting Hired 137

Profile: Janet Brand. 137

Evaluating Your Appropriate Experience and Skills 138

Hone Your Pre-Interview Skills. 139

Study Real Estate Listings 140
Finding Your Niche 141
Finding Real Estate Job Openings 142
Acing the Interview 143

Chapter 9

Getting Ahead 149

Profile: Jean Warkala 149
How to Excel in Real Estate and
    Move to the Next Level 151
Using Timelines and Benchmarks to
    Keep Your Career on Track 168

Chapter 10

Opening Your Own Real Estate Office 171

Profile: Beverly Fairchild 171
Starting with a Business Plan 175
The Business Plan 176
Staffing 184
Franchises 186
Franchise Start-Up Costs 188
Buying an Established Real Estate Firm 189

Resources 191

Glossary 203

Index 213

Acknowledgments

I would like to thank my editors Jen Dorsey and Karen Thomas at Entrepreneur Press as well as Jack Savage and Cheryl Kimball. I would also like to thank the following real estate professionals who helped me put this book together and provided their personal stories and their wisdom:

- David Fischer of Bank of America and Bloomfish LLC, Atlanta, Georgia
- Sandra Ferrantello, Licensed by Coldwell Banker in Pennsylvania
- Ed Grossman, Broker at Weichert Realtors in Monroe, New York
- Barbara Tremain, Houlihan Lawrence office, Katonah, New York
- Carol Mayer, Broker, Houlihan Lawrence, White Plains, New York

- Jo Falcone, Office Manager, Century 21 Wolff, White Plains, New York
- Janet Brand, Associate Broker at Houlihan Lawrence in Briarcliff Manor, New York
- Susan Berman of the Houlihan Lawrence office, Katonah, New York
- Henry Munneke of the Terry Business School, Atlanta, Georgia
- Walter Sanford of Sanford Systems & Strategies, Kankakee, Illinois
- John Galletta of Prudential Real Estate, Greenwich, Connecticut
- Betsy Fairchild and Renee Collins of Collins Morrow Real Estate, New Fairfield, Connecticut

Preface

Real estate is such an immense subject that there are few true experts in the overall field. Buying and selling residential or commercial real estate, selling raw land, managing or investing in properties, or putting money into real estate investment trusts (REITs) are just a few of the ways in which people become involved in this complex industry. What makes the real estate industry so vast and difficult to master is that every state, city, and town has its own laws and ordinances—and that's just in the United States. Internationally, real estate takes on entirely different implications. Just try to buy a chateau in France or a villa in Switzerland.

My own involvement in real estate first started, as is the case for most people, when I bought a home. Suddenly I was learning about a subject I knew nothing about. Yet, each time

I thought I was flying across that learning curve, there was something new to discover.

When my wife and I walked out of the closing process, keys in hand to our new home, we were both far more knowledgeable about real estate than when we first spoke to a real estate agent and asked her to simply help us find the type of home we wanted. While I didn't see myself making a career move into real estate, I did understand immediately that it was a field rich with intriguing possibilities. With that in mind, I decided to do some research and soon I wrote some short articles on investing in real estate. However, it was an article that I wrote for *Westchester Magazine*, the premier magazine of Westchester County, New York, that piqued my interest in the field. The article was all about undiscovered affordable neighborhoods. Not only did I find several terrific neighborhoods, but I also forged relationships with a number of realtors. Each had his or her own reason for getting into the field and each had a passion for what he or she did. I quickly realized that the people who made up the real estate business were as diverse as the industry itself.

When it came to writing a book about getting into the field, I was excited about talking to these agents and meeting other people all throughout the industry. Being a "people person" myself, and having conducted hundreds of interviews as an author and journalist, I was enthusiastic about digging deeper into the world of real estate and further talking to the realtors I had met along the way as well as others that I look forward to meeting. There was great enthusiasm from everyone with whom I spoke, including one of the top residential sellers in the nation and a 23-year-old who had already opened his own development business with several homes purchased. Although their backgrounds and motivation were different, it was clear that these were people who had chosen a career that they really loved.

About the Book

Before embarking on a career in real estate, it is worthwhile to take a glimpse at how the field has emerged into the multi-billion dollar industry it is today. You will also want to take some time to determine whether it is a field that would fit your personality and lifestyle. The first two chapters will brief you on real estate history and then let you self-evaluate your potential future in the field.

From there, you will get an overview of what you will need to learn, and how you can advance in the field, which includes many types of employment opportunities. The middle chapters examine the nuts and bolts of the job, including the environment and responsibilities of a real estate professional. Attention is then turned to internships, mentoring, and interviews as ways to break into the field. And finally, you will take a look down the road at ways to get ahead once you are truly in the field. Perhaps you will own your own real estate firm in the future. You never know.

Like anyone weighing options before starting in a new career, you'll want to have plenty of data available, and with that in mind, several references are listed at the back of the book which provide additional information about the real estate industry.

Having talked to numerous full-time real estate professionals and learned first-hand what their typical days, nights, and weekends are like, I smile whenever I hear someone say, "maybe I'll dabble in real estate," or "I could see doing real estate on the side." Real estate is a career to which you must make a full commitment. If you do, it can be exciting, lucrative, and very rewarding.

Good luck!

All About
Real Estate

In her sixth year in the real estate business, Susan Berman enjoys her career working for the Houlihan Lawrence office in Katonah, New York. Originally in jewelry design, Susan opted to go into real estate because she wanted a career in which she would not have to make a long commute and she could utilize her people skills. She had also gained insight into the real estate business when she and her husband had sold their first home in North Salem, New York. They

had bought land and built a custom home and then learned that selling such a "personalized" house was difficult.

After taking the 45 hours of state-required course work at a nearby school, Susan passed her New York State licensing exam. While still taking her course, she looked into employment opportunities. In fact, she approached an agent in a neighboring town, with whom she was quite familiar and asked if he would take her on as an agent once she got her license. He said yes, and she worked for this small real estate company for two years. The firm had offices in more than one town, so she worked two days in each of the two areas, both of which were close to home.

"Sphere of influence is a big part of this job," explained Susan, referring to knowing people in the towns, having contacts, and being confident in her ability to get things done. "I also set aside time to know the market," she adds, referring to the local real estate market in the two towns where she was working.

While working in the area, she got to know an agent in the Katonah Houlihan Lawrence office, who introduced her to the office manager, and they set up a time to talk. "I explained that I had some experience in this area since I had been living here for three years," says Susan, who was then hired and switched to the larger company.

"There is a big difference in the amount of support, and the potential for business is greater in a larger office," says Susan about moving up to a larger firm. "They can do more advertising and, therefore, they will get a greater volume of customers."

In her three years at Houlihan Lawrence, she has seen a steady growth in her income due to the number of homes she has sold. While taking ongoing continuing education classes, as is necessary according to state law, Susan works a full week. Although the hours vary, she is comfortable with the flexibility necessary to succeed in this business. "It's the kind of thing where you're on call all the time," explains Susan. "You could start at 7 A.M. one day or have a typical nine-to-five day another."

According to Susan Berman, the key factors for success in this business are having the right type of personality and a fair amount of social grace. "I think it's most important to be reassuring and not hard-edged. People like someone who is low key and knows it's a business. You also need to be organized and on top of things," she adds.

■　　■　　■

From the northeastern tip of Maine to the Mexican border in Southern California, you will find real estate: single-family homes, apartment complexes, industrial parks, office buildings, retail outlets, factories, strip malls, indoor malls, farmland, golf courses, tracts of raw land, vast acres of wildlife habitat, and much more. You would, in fact, have a difficult time finding a parcel of land that is not accounted for, in some way—as property of a state, municipality, corporation, private landowner, or, like the national parks, the federal government. All are real estate. And many are of interest to real estate professionals.

Today, computers and other high-tech tools assist real estate professionals and provide numerous vantage points for viewing and studying land, finding detailed documentation in seconds, calculating land mass, acreage, and square footage, and helping in many other ways. Yet, despite the new technology and the wealth of information available on properties and neighborhoods, the basics remain the same: People want to own or rent homes in which they feel comfortable, and both companies and individuals need places from which to conduct their businesses.

Throughout this book, you will explore how to become part of the real estate profession, one that grows and expands and has billions of dollars in transactions each year. However, before delving into the hows and whys of becoming a real estate professional, this chapter looks briefly at the history of real estate in the United States and how it has changed over the years.

History

From the days of the earliest settlers, ownership of land has been important in the development of the United States. As early settlements arose in the 16th and 17th centuries along the Atlantic coast, land sales were an important part of American history. Despite the lack of sellers agreements, and commission payments, the first well-known real estate deal was the one in which Peter Minuet purchased the island of Manhattan from Native Americans for $24 worth of goods. Of course, the Indians were not actually living there at the time.

Ownership of land was among the primary goals of settlers who came to the New World. Many were seeking freedom and independence, primarily from Great Britain where many had been displaced from the land. In North America, the immigrants settled on tracts acquired through either battles or agreements with Native Americans. In the north, family farms emerged, whereas much larger plantations were spread across the southeastern states. However, land ownership was quickly becoming the right of the wealthy. By the time the Revolutionary War ended, significant tracts of land were owned by a relatively small number of very wealthy individuals. While such land barons rented and sometimes sold plots of land, at the end of the 18th century a growing number of laborers in the northeastern cities were also seeking to make their dreams of land ownership come true.

The Homestead Act

It was newspaper publisher Horace Greely who in 1837 wrote "Go west young man, go forth into the country," in hopes of encouraging those seeking land to head west and buy their own tracts of land. Although the government was only charging slightly over a dollar per acre, this was still too much for most workers to pay for the acres necessary to start a farm. The laborers voiced their discontent and the result, some 25 years later (government moved slowly even at that time), was the passage of the Homestead Act. This important act mandated that any adult citizen who farmed land provided by the federal government for a specified period of time could eventually own 160 acres of land. The Homestead Act opened up more than 300 million acres to new landowners and resulted in rapid growth westward. As the number of landowners increased, selling, trading, or leasing land became more common and the concept of an emerging real estate industry expanded west along with the new frontier.

The early 20th century saw the United States changing from a mostly agricultural nation to a country with major manufacturing cities, and not only in the northeast. Chicago led the midwestern cities and grew to be one of the largest cities in the world. In fact, half of the population of the United States was living in cities by the early 1920s. However, as cities grew, property values also grew, pushing many people out of the cities to emerging suburban communities. As railroads and the automobile made it easier to travel to and from the big cities, families were able to find more affordable housing in these peripheral areas. In the early 1900s, the real estate industry was booming in the major cities, where commercial real estate was being purchased to satisfy the growth of industry and retail businesses. More than 100 skyscrapers were built in New York and Chicago in the 1920s.

Unfortunately, the Roaring 20s came to an end with the Great Depression, and the real estate industry sank along with the hopes of millions of Americans looking forward to future prosperity. Real estate values plummeted, and the federal government was called upon to help the beleaguered real estate industry.

The Creation of the Federal Housing Administration

In 1934, the Federal Housing Administration (FHA) was formed in an effort to save the struggling residential real estate industry. Few people could afford to purchase homes, and those who could were only offered mortgage loans for 50 percent of the value of their homes. In addition, such loans had to be repaid within five years. Since these were the best terms lenders could offer, homebuilding all but stopped. As a result, several million construction workers and laborers in related industries became unemployed. By the mid-1930s, 60 percent of the U.S. population was not even thinking about home owning; they were renting and trying to cover their rent payments. Landlords were not faring well either;

they were often unable to cover their own loans because many renters were out of work and fell behind in their payments.

In an effort to decrease the risk related to real estate loans and make it easier for banks to structure more favorable terms to potential homebuyers, the Federal Housing Administration provided mortgage insurance. This meant that banks would incur less risk against homeowners defaulting on loans. FHA-approved lenders were then insured on mortgages for single and multifamily homes. Obviously, the FHA mortgage insurance proved to be a boost to the real estate industry. Some 33 million home mortgages have been insured by the FHA.

Post-War Expansion and the Emergence of the Suburbs

The growth of the real estate business was spurred on by a major demand for housing and the construction of highways in the years after World War II. Federal funds no longer needed for the war effort went to constructing more than 40,000 miles of highways, which led to a significant increase in automobile ownership and travel. More highways and more cars meant that housing could be developed in previously hard-to-reach areas. As a result, the suburbs grew rapidly in the years between 1945 and 1960. New housing developments emerged all over the nation, many as new homes for war veterans who returned from overseas and became first-time homeowners thanks to the GI bill, which allowed veterans to buy homes with no money down. In addition, the GI bill guaranteed the loans, removing the risk for lenders. Low-cost, long-term mortgages soon became available to non-veterans as well, and the nation prospered with the building of numerous apartment buildings and complexes in the burgeoning new suburbs. Homes sold at an incredible rate. The percentage of homeowners in the United States jumped from around 40 percent in 1940 to over 60 percent by 1960. The new highways and the proliferation of homeowners also drew retailers to these rapidly expanding neighborhoods, and shopping centers and strip malls began to appear on the suburban landscape.

More Homes, More Brokers

Filling the thousands of new homes and apartments also meant that many new real estate offices opened, and the suburban real estate professionals of the 1950s were very busy. Being a real estate agent in a housing boom was very profitable for those with good sales skills, and compared to today, there were fewer guidelines, less paperwork, and deals closed more quickly. The post-war homes were brand new, so there were fewer concerns about the condition of the properties. School districts were not evaluated as they are today, and far less data was available to homebuyers.

To help the brokers and agents sell homes, the Multiple Listing Service (MLS) was established in 1952. In this era before computer technology, the MLS was printed weekly on loose-leaf paper and provided basic information regarding each home for sale. Agents using the new service were immediately ahead of their competitors.

Fair Housing Laws

One of the problems that persisted even after the housing boom of the 1950s and early 1960s was discrimination. There remained a great disparity in the number of white homeowners versus minority homeowners, especially people of color. In an attempt to rectify this situation, the Fair Housing Act was passed in 1968. Unfortunately, it took many years before there was any actual enforcement of these laws. Even today, although discrimination is less obvious, there remains a significant disparity in the value of homes owned by white homeowners and those owned by immigrants, minorities, and people of color.

From Local Real Estate Agents to Big Business

Throughout the housing boom of the 1950s, local real estate agents working in privately owned real estate firms handled the bulk of transactions. Local brokers had their share of neighborhood listings, and their jobs were simply to sell the properties in their areas. Spreading the word meant finding your own means of advertising, which was often through local newspapers, fliers, signs, and word-of-mouth. Mom and pop real estate outfits remained the norm into the 1960s, but

SINGER SEWING CENTERS

For those with a penchant for history, it was actually the Singer Sewing Centers, which evolved after the invention of the sewing machine in the mid-1800s, that could be considered a forerunner of the franchise businesses we've come to recognize in nearly every town and city in the country. Singer gathered salesmen and dealers in the late-1800s from different regions of the country who were interested in selling the machines. Singer made written contract agreements with the salesmen and dealers to sell Singer products. The contracts became the basis for modern-day franchise agreements. When the sewing centers opened in the early 1900s, they were run as franchise businesses.

as the decade neared an end, the business climate was beginning to change.

The emergence of the franchise in the late 1960s would soon have a major impact upon various areas in the economy. As television grew from an entertainment medium to a fixture in our culture, this new means of mass marketing (through national advertising) helped promote franchise companies in a way that had not been anticipated.

Through the franchise, corporations saw opportunities to spread a business formula from coast to coast by licensing, thus enabling local business owners to buy into a franchise and own a business under the umbrella of the larger company. This encouraged many entrepreneurs to start up a business with less risk than going out on their own. The franchise led to rapid expansion of businesses in many industries, including real estate. Century 21 Real Estate Corporation, formed in Orange County, California, by real estate brokers Art Bartlett and Marsh Fisher, was among the earliest real estate franchises and is now one of the largest, along with ERA, Prudential, and RE/MAX.

PROFILE
RE/MAX

RE/MAX, one of the leading real estate companies in the world, was founded in 1973 by Dave and Gail Liniger, two real estate agents in Denver, Colorado. They were concerned about the fact that office owners controlled the jobs of salespeople and that the companies took 50 percent of the agents' commissions. At that time, there was a high turnover rate in real estate as many agents left the business in less than three years. The Linigers put together a business plan that they hoped would serve to inspire both agents and company owners to succeed and called it RE/MAX, short for Real Estate Maximums. Their plan was to have agents work together as individual contractors, pooling resources and paying a set fee to the company each month. This gave agents their freedom while providing the franchise company with steady income. It was a benefit to those who were serious about their careers and knew how to sell because they could now cover the fee to the company without having to worry about giving up half their commissions.

Apparently this idea to create offices in which both agents and owners would benefit caught on. Today, some 33 years later, the company is global, with 5,000 offices and over 100,000 agents. RE/MAX franchises business opportunities and provides full training for agents and personnel.

Residential sales make up the majority of RE/MAX sales transactions, but commercial sales, relocation, and real estate auctions are also part of the business. With a colorful hot-air balloon as its logo, RE/MAX now has the largest fleet of hot air balloons in the world.

■   ■   ■

Because real estate did not require a formula product such as the Big Mac, or a standard room layout such as Holiday Inn, franchise companies in the real estate industry were able to purchase existing real estate firms and bring them into the fold. The large franchise companies could advertise nationally, establish and run a mass training program, and use the growing technology to their advantage. For the help and guidance they could offer the franchisees, the company would get its cut of all transactions. Of course, not all companies went the franchise route, but clearly, big business was able to step in and take control of a major chunk of the real estate industry.

The Real Estate Market

Through the many years of land and property sales in the United States, a vast and complex real estate industry has evolved. As is typically the case in any sales-oriented industry, supply and demand influence the price of the goods available and services offered. Therefore, when supply increases and many properties or tracts of land are for sale, the prices go down and you have a buyers market. Conversely, when there are fewer available properties and land is scarce, prices rise, and the market favors the sellers, who can demand top dollar.

Over the years, the market has fluctuated in step with economic conditions, and as any long-time real estate professional will agree, it can be a bumpy ride with roller coaster ups and downs. Unlike other goods and services, which can be transported to balance low supply and high demand, real estate cannot. Real estate remains unique in that a given area can buck the national trend. Despite a soft market, a specific area can remain in demand because of limited space to build or limited resources. This explains why certain areas saw housing prices continue to rise even as the economy staggered in recent years.

Factors that affect the supply and demand of real estate include fiscal policies and taxes at the federal, state, and local levels. For example, in an area where there are few homes available, and prices could be high (in a sellers market), significant property taxes may limit the seller from getting top dollar, even if the homes are in demand. Construction and labor costs, demographics, local employment, economic factors, mass transportation, roads and access, geography, topography, natural disasters, and the rise or fall of population in a given area may also have an effect on a given real estate market. In the end, however, as the overall national population grows and people live longer, real estate will usually be a sound investment over time.

The Industry Today

Real estate is a multibillion-dollar industry in the United States, and despite economic downturns, it still continues to grow quickly in many parts of the country. The median price of a single-family American home hit $188,800 at the end of the first quarter of 2005, a rise of 9.7 percent compared with a year earlier. As of 2005, there were approximately five million people employed in some aspect of the industry, with 10 percent, or about 500,000, working as agents or brokers.

Technology has changed the face of the industry; easy access to detailed data and virtual tours allow buyers to view homes without passing over the thresholds. Technology, however, is only a tool for research, listings, and storing, generating, and calculating data. The business remains a people industry, because people need to determine where, when, and why they want to buy or sell a property. The human factor is why no two real estate deals are identical and why you need to approach each transaction from a unique perspective.

The government continues to monitor the real estate industry closely, particularly in regard to the Fair Housing Act and other fair housing practices. It is still difficult, however, to curtail "habits" such as steering, when agents steer specific groups of people into specific areas.

Debate continues on the responsibilities of real estate brokers and agents. Even in the modern era, with new technology and plenty of regulations, guidelines, and documents to uphold the laws, gray areas still remain. For example, situations of dual representation whereby agents represent both buyers and sellers continue to be a source of debate. In our litigious society, modern real estate agents and/or brokers need to protect themselves and their clients as much as possible. Waivers, disclaimers, disclosure forms, and numerous other pieces of paperwork are commonplace today and designed to provide such protection. Real estate law is definitely worth studying because the days of "buyer beware" have become the days of "agent and broker" beware.

Nonetheless, while there are various issues and trends that need to be addressed from both a governmental and societal viewpoint, real estate remains a constantly growing field with classes filling up every day and new licenses being granted on a steady basis. There are potential fortunes to be made in the real estate industry by proactive, well-trained agents and brokers who have the desire to work hard and keep a finger on the pulse of the industry.

CHAPTER 2

Is Real Estate the
Right Career for You?

PROFILE
John Galletta
New Agent

John Galletta has been a real estate agent for just over one year and is building his business slowly and steadily. Working from the Greenwich office of Prudential Connecticut Real Estate, he has utilized his involvement in his kids' school as a means of networking. He found a niche with people relocating to the area, often from outside of the country, and renting apartments. "I'm working mostly with buyers, or in this case, renters right now," explains Galletta, who is one of

1,000 real estate agents in Greenwich, although unlike Galletta, many are part timers. "It's very competitive, but I'm building up my own list of contacts," says Galletta, who is looking at specific demographic groups and avoids the cold calling and mass marketing approach.

He has also found that it is not always easy aligning with more senior agents because time is money and they simply cannot take such time out to help hone newer agents. Instead, he has aligned with another agent who has been in the business slightly longer and is also still building her career. They are able to help and learn from each other as they establish themselves.

Galletta, whose background includes working at J.P. Morgan and Standard & Poor in the financial industry, appreciates being closer to home and family and no longer having to wake up at the crack of dawn to make the long commute to lower Manhattan. "I like being able to use my skills in the local environment with more flexible hours," adds Galletta, who feels good about his first year in the business.

■   ■   ■

There are two types of people that attempt to go into a profession. First, there are those who learn the profession by the numbers and proceed "by the book." Then there are those who not only learn the nuts and bolts of the profession, but also possess, or develop, an innate feel for what is taking place under the surface. For example, a dedicated student can get his postgraduate degree in psychology and have a thorough grasp of theories but may not understand what is truly going on with the patient sitting in his office. Likewise, a good chef can create a recipe based on her knowledge of flavor combinations. A great chef, however, just knows just what to add to a dish to make it sumptuous. The same holds true with real estate. One real agent can meet the needs of a client by finding a home with the right number of rooms, on a quiet street, with a two-car garage, and within the price range of the prospective buyer. However, he or she will then be frustrated when the family says it's just not quite right for them.

The real estate agent with a "feel" for what a client wants, beyond that which is in the listings, will have a feel for the right houses to show clients. He will be able to establish a rapport with buyers or sellers and know what they are truly seeking. Although you can succeed in real estate by doing everything by the book, you can succeed to a far greater extent, and also enjoy your work much more, by developing a deeper understanding of what your customers really want.

To develop such an understanding you will need to have a passion for the business. It is that passion and that desire that will have you reading articles on your own time, looking at online real estate newsletters, discussing and learning the business from seasoned pros, and getting to know your customers beyond the type of house, office or retail location they

are seeking. You will establish a rapport with customers and gain insight into their goals and needs as individuals.

Along with developing a knack for understanding the needs of your customers, the modern day real estate agent needs to have a diverse knowledge base. Although you do not need to be an expert in all of these areas, you will want to have a working knowledge of many topics, including:

- The state of the real estate industry
- Market trends in your area
- Property taxes
- State and local taxes
- Variances
- Real estate law
- Zoning ordinances
- School reports
- Crime statistics
- Garbage disposal
- Septic tanks
- Architecture
- Decorating
- Lawn care and maintenance
- Home security
- Square footage and how it is determined
- Deeds and land holdings
- Local cable and telephone providers

A real estate agent also needs to be able to do plenty of research and ultimately be confident in her ability to present a home, office, or other type of property with appropriate knowledge. Real estate buyers today are savvy, so they know what they are looking for and are ready with numerous questions. A good agent will be ready with answers or know where to find the answers quickly. In fact, most successful real estate agents have answers to many of the potential buyer's questions at the ready, before he asks them. They become experts on properties and their locations. If you've ever traveled through a neighborhood with a real estate agent representing that area, you'll find that it is almost like having your own tour guide. The agent can tell you all sorts of information about each and every aspect of the community and about the houses, stores, and/or office buildings you pass. Real estate agents sell neighborhoods to their clients because, after all, people don't just buy a home or a business location. They buy locations, neighborhoods.

The question is, could this person be you?

How Do You Like to Spend Your Day?

If you enjoy the comfort of a quiet office where you can close the door and complete your daily workload, then real estate is clearly not for you. The person who enjoys the comfort of a structured nine-to-five routine is not typically a real estate agent.

If, however, you enjoy spending a good portion of your day outside of the office environment, you might be better suited for a real estate career. Although there will inevitably be many hours spent in the office, the individual who enjoys being mobile during the day is more likely to enjoy this career.

A real estate agent needs to understand that from day to day her schedule will differ. In fact, as the day proceeds, the schedule will change based on the needs of the clients, the availability of the properties you are showing, and the necessary research that needs to be done to answer client questions. If you are comfortable creating your own schedule and flexible enough to recognize that your schedule may change often, then you have the right mind-set for real estate.

Are You a People Person?

The term *people person* is widely used—but rarely defined and can vary some by industry. In real estate, it means being able to establish a comfortable rapport with each client. It also means being able to communicate effectively with a wide variety of personality types. No, you do not have to be the extremely extroverted "life of the party." You do, however, need to be able to express yourself with confidence and make other people feel comfortable in your presence.

The key to doing this, as any good people person will agree, is not simply talking to other people, but more significantly, knowing how to listen and process what the other person is saying. A people person takes in, and responds to, other people's needs and concerns. Many people will tell you that they are very comfortable talking to other people, but are they comfortable talking *with* other people? Do they understand what the other person is trying to say? Do they have an idea of what the other person is thinking or feeling? The person who is comfortable both talking and listening to other people is a true people person. Are you that person?

Three cautions about being a people person:

1. Don't assume that you "know" a person based on preconceived ideas.
2. Don't jump to conclusions about other people based on limited information.
3. Don't use your people skills to manipulate others.

Is Research Your Thing?

You might not have spent your free time in the library during college, but it is more likely that you will succeed as a real estate agent if you are familiar with doing research. When it comes to due diligence, there are people who enjoy digging for facts and uncovering information. Conversely, there are those who hate the whole idea of sifting through records or files.

In today's real estate industry, in order to come up with background information on properties and answer the questions of prospective buyers you absolutely *must* be able to perform due diligence by doing research both online and in libraries or courthouses. The internet is a godsend to real estate agents, putting a wealth of information at the fingertips of brokers and agents. Of course, it is not the final answer. Dusty deeds and dirty documents in old filing cabinets at the courthouse or in the basement of the local hall of records are also part of due diligence. There is no way around the need to do the legwork, or homework, in this field. While a title can usually be found through a title search company, there may be permits and various other documents that need to be found to verify information about a property.

Keep in mind that while the internet is a great tool for real estate agents, it is also at the fingertips of the buyers and sellers, providing them with a great deal of current market information. Therefore, you have to stay on top of the latest data to be up-to-date when customers ask questions or make reference to materials that they have found. Many agents become too comfortable with a few industry real estate web sites and forget the big picture. It is advantageous to visit a wide variety of real estate sites to get an overall feel for the industry.

Can You Sell?

Real estate is, in part, a sales job. Although some agents specialize in commercial and other types of real estate, the vast majority of agents throughout the country are selling homes. To sell successfully, you typically need to have a product that you believe in, a price point that is fair, and a competitive edge that makes your product better than others. In addition, you need to pay attention to what the buyer wants. Real estate is no exception.

If you are representing the seller, you need to firmly believe that you can sell her property. You also need to make sure it is priced and listed accordingly. When you sell, you want to accentuate the positives that you believe give this house the competitive edge over all others that prospective buyers will be seeing. Finally, you need to pay attention to what the buyer is seeking. For example, if a family is seeking an eat-in kitchen, ample closet space, and a good-sized backyard, your focus should not be on the paneling in the den, stained glass windows, or the view. Selling in the modern age means finding a good fit rather than trying to convince someone that you have what she wants, even if it is not the case. Full disclosure is as necessary to protect the agent as it is to protect the seller.

Representing a buyer is also a matter of finding the right fit. The best you can do is to guide prospective buyers to homes you feel meet their needs. The art of selling in this case is subtler than in years gone by because the high-pressure sales approach typically does not work. People won't buy a house because you've pressured them into it, after all, it's not exactly an impulse buy. As many real estate agents will agree, you can try hard to find everything on the prospective buyer's wish list, but you cannot factor in the intangibles.

The "hard sell" in the real estate industry today is more closely acquainted with late night television hawkers and the online scammers who offer real estate get-rich-quick schemes and appear to have all the answers as they walk that tightrope between ethics and unscrupulous behavior. There are some legitimate top players in the business who have used aggressive systems, remained ethical, and made a fortune. They are, however, the exceptions. Be careful if you find yourself following a real estate guru.

To sell successfully in an often skeptical, litigious society, where your clients have plenty of data available at their fingertips and the phone number of the local Better Business Bureau on their speed dialers, you need to utilize your most valuable qualities as a salesperson, such as being honest, sincere, and personable. As one real estate agent puts it, "you need to remember courtesy, which is almost a lost art today."

Like other sales-oriented professions, real estate relies heavily on return business, but not in the same manner. A shoe store will likely operate on the 80–20 principle, where 80 percent of business comes from return customers, while 20 percent comes from new customers. It is unlikely that 80 percent of homebuyers will return to you to buy their next homes unless they are moving frequently or you stay in the business for many years. However, it is likely that a large percentage of your business will come from friends and family members of your satisfied clients. Therefore, if you sell a home for one customer and she was pleased with the deal and your manner of doing business, it is possible that you can go on to sell every house on that block through referrals. Although the percentage will probably not be 80 percent, a large number of your clients will come from referrals, so remember the significance of establishing relationships if you want to succeed.

How Do You Feel about Flexible Hours?

There is a common misconception that real estate is a nice part-time career in which you can dabble without having to put in too many hours. Most real estate agents will smile and tell you that those individuals who believe that they can "dabble" and succeed are fooling themselves. A career in real estate, as in any field, takes commitment and dedication, and that means investing a substantial amount of time and energy. Like most jobs, it means being in the office regularly and working at least 30 to 40 hours a week, sometimes more.

Therefore, having flexible hours in real estate does not mean choosing which two or three days to work. Instead, it refers to having flexible hours from day to day. Typically, in most offices, each agent is required to put in a certain number of office hours manning the phones. This can be a regularly scheduled number of hours on a specific day or it can vary from week to week, depending on the office. Beyond that, you will need the flexibility to meet customers after their nine-to-five days have ended or to show open houses on weekends.

Most real estate agents are on call much of the time. Although you do not need to completely sacrifice your social life, you do need to approach your career with the mind-set that you may be working on Saturday or Sunday afternoons. If you are used to looking at your watch and waiting patiently for five o'clock to signal the end of the workday, or if you resent the idea of working on the weekend, then this is not the career for you.

Of course, it often takes the former nine-to-fiver a little while to adjust to a schedule where she is at home all day on a Tuesday and working for five hours on a Saturday. A flexible schedule is a must for most real estate agents.

Are You Proactive?

Billions of dollars change hands every year in real estate transactions. However, nearly 90 percent of the commissions from such transactions go to the top 10 percent producers. This is because there are real estate agents and brokers, and then there are super real estate agents and brokers. It is unlikely that you will become the next Donald Trump, but you can build a highly lucrative real estate career by taking matters into your own hands and developing a system of lead generation and marketing that works for you. The successful real estate agents are the ones that "make things happen" by putting themselves in the right place at the right time, finding angles, and developing systems that set them apart from their many competitors.

Being proactive in real estate means researching and generating leads. It means finding the right demographic groups and reaching out to potential sellers through strategic marketing efforts. It means marketing yourself to anyone you believe may be a potential customer or to anyone you believe can lead you to a potential seller or buyer. It means evaluating what buyers want and finding such properties. It means spending time carefully analyzing the market and promoting yourself and what you can do for people looking to buy or sell property.

Not everyone will excel in this area, but to be an independent contractor, you need to make things happen. If you are not good at self-motivation, making calls and getting your day started, it will be hard for you to build your sphere of influence, circle of contacts, and ultimately, your customer base.

What Skills and Abilities Do You Need?

Flexibility, perseverance, stamina, motivation, and the ability to solve problems are among the most important skills necessary for a real estate career. The real estate field today is highly competitive and being able to find what you need quickly can make or break a sale. Research skills and computer skills are essential, and organizational skills are also a must. Multitasking also helps. It may be a much overused term, but when you are waiting for one customer to show up, on the phone with another, and pulling up listings on your computer for a third, you will be glad you have the ability to multitask.

Other skills and attributes you may want to master, or at least add to your repertoire include:

- *Tact and diplomacy.*
- *The ability to remember names and faces.*
- *Good number skills.* Or you should have the ability to give ballpark estimates.
- *Driving skills.* It may sound silly, but clients want to concentrate on the houses you are showing them and not on arriving in one piece. It also helps to have a good sense of direction.
- *Communication skills.* Whether it is a pleasant phone manner or a polite e-mail, you need to know how to communicate effectively both verbally and in writing.
- *The ability to juggle schedules.* You may have a day filled with appointments, but as soon as you fall an hour behind, your entire day may be in jeopardy. Learn to juggle.
- *A sense of humor.* Customers may be tense. After all, they are in the process of buying or selling a home. Being able to break the tension with appropriate humor or appreciate a customer's humor is important when establishing a comfortable working relationship.
- *The ability to listen.* This means hearing what people say and reading unspoken signals such as body language and/or facial expressions.

Integration of a variety of skills is all part and parcel of a real estate agent's typical day. One of the most enjoyable features of the job, according to several real estate agents, is that you get to use a mixed bag of skills, some of which you would not be able to apply to other careers. For this reason, many people who have worked in the corporate world opt to go into the real estate field. They say the corporate world did not allow them to utilize more than a few of their skills or abilities, but real estate allows them to tap into many of them.

Do You Have the "Real Estate" Personality?

The real estate personality is one that combines the characteristics of a variety of other careers. Agents will tell you that they play roles from tour guides to researchers to psychologists while handling duties that range from hard and fast negotiating to reassuring hand holding.

Being an outgoing person is just one preferred personality trait. Brokers look for agents who are also pleasant, upbeat, compassionate, and honest. Ironically, customers look for the same qualities. Unless someone is buying and selling homes strictly as investment vehicles, personality is typically a factor in selecting a real estate agent for most buyers and sellers. The mere size and scope of buying or selling a home has many emotional implications. Therefore, how you interact with customers will be very important, and your personality will become part of the equation.

Use Figure 2.1 to see if you have the right stuff to be a real estate agent. Once you have assessed your own abilities, capabilities, personal skills, and personality traits, you can determine whether you want to pursue a career in real estate. If you determine that this is a field of interest, you will then need to start learning the business. Training, education, and finding a job in the field are all discussed in the next chapters.

FIGURE 2.1
Self-Test for Aptitude and Attitude
Do You Fit In? Do You Have What It Takes?

Answer yes or no to the following 15 questions. Be honest, since this is a personal assessment.

1. I listen to people when they talk and ask questions if I need more information. ❏ Yes ❏ No

2. I am comfortable talking with people I do not know. ❏ Yes ❏ No

3. I do well with a flexible schedule. ❏ Yes ❏ No

4. I have no problem walking away from a situation (such as a seller asking an unrealistic price) that I do not feel is promising. ❏ Yes ❏ No

5. I am very good at self-generating and self-motivating.

   ❑ Yes ❑ No

6. Being a good salesperson is my strongest asset in real estate.
   ❑ Yes ❑ No

7. I work best in an environment that is consistent from day to
   day. ❑ Yes ❑ No

8. My technical/computer skills are very strong. ❑ Yes ❑ No

9. If I do not have the answer to a question, I usually know
   where to find it. ❑ Yes ❑ No

10. When I promise a client something, it gets done on time.

    ❑ Yes ❑ No

11. I take a proactive approach to business, seeking it rather than
    waiting for it to come to me. ❑ Yes ❑ No

12. I am comfortable in negotiations. ❑ Yes ❑ No

13. I believe in full disclosure, but only to a point. ❑ Yes ❑ No

14. I am extremely comfortable showing people around my neigh-
    borhood. ❑ Yes ❑ No

15. By using a hard sales technique, I can demonstrate my confi-
    dence in the product (or property in this case). ❑ Yes ❑ No

Scoring

The best answer to questions 1 through 5, 8 through 12 and 14 is YES.

The best answer for questions 6, 7, 13, and 15 is NO.

Score based on those answers, giving yourself 1 point for each best answer.

If you've scored over 12, you are of the right mind-set to go into real estate.

A score of 9 through 11, means you have the potential but need to adjust your thinking in some areas.

A score of 6 through 8 means you will have to refocus and approach real estate with a different outlook.

A score under 6 may mean that real estate is not for you or that it will be a challenge to meet the physical and psychological criteria necessary.

■   ■   ■

Training, Education, **and Background**

PROFILE

James Taylor Lott

In the spring of 2005, James Taylor Lott was wrapping up his real estate education at Terry College of Business at the University of Georgia. He majored in both commercial real estate and finance. His training ground is now at Sun Trust Bank in Atlanta, where for the next year he will be learning about structuring real estate deals, pricing loans, writing credit memos, doing home inspections, and much more. In the end, he is heading toward a real estate career as a lender to homebuilders. For now he is taking in as much as he can about the real estate business in Atlanta, one of the nation's most thriving markets.

Along with studying real estate in the classroom and doing fieldwork, he has also been trained informally by his family. "My dad was in commercial real estate and his dad was in real estate," explains Lott, making him a third generation real estate professional in the state of Georgia.

Lott appreciates the value of his real estate education. "I want to learn as much as I can about the industry estate while I'm young," he says. Although he is just out of one of the top real estate programs in the nation (ranked in the top five), he is already well-versed on the local real estate scene. "A lot of places have national home building, but in this area there are many smaller builders, companies building 20 to 70 homes a year," he notes, adding that the market has branched outward from the heart of Atlanta and is now starting to move back inward as some of the older homes, closer to the downtown area, are being fixed up and gaining in value.

As James continues to educate himself in real estate, like many of his recent alumni, he hopes to own and develop properties down the road.

■   ■   ■

Real estate laws vary widely throughout the 50 states, course and licensing requirements also differ from state to state. However, the basic principles and fundamentals of selling real estate remain essentially the same. The necessary paperwork and regulations vary, but you still need to know how to interact with clients, calculate commissions, use a multiple listing service, understand the latest state and federal real estate laws, and conduct business in an ethical manner at all times.

There are numerous accredited real estate schools in each state plus additional schools providing online education. Depending on the state requirements, you may be taking anywhere from 45 to 120 hours of course credits before graduating and taking your licensing exam. The maximum time for taking such a course load also varies but is typically three to six months. The cost for the license courses is generally between $200 and $600, depending on the number of state-required hours and the history and reputation of the school. Most states also require you be sponsored by a broker before taking the licensing exam.

According to the United States Department of Labor, in all states, as well as in the District of Columbia, both real estate sales agents and brokers must be high school graduates and over the age of 18 years.

Real Estate Courses: What to Expect

Real estate courses include all of the basics for understanding how real estate transactions work. Course work can include:

- Real estate laws
- Forms of real estate ownership
- State principles of real estate
- Real estate listings
- Leases
- Real estate taxes and other liens
- Real estate appraisal
- Understanding contracts
- Transfer of title
- Disclosures
- Deeds and title records
- Methods of real estate financing
- Commissions
- Fair housing and ethical practices
- Environmental issues
- The real estate transaction

These are among the many areas that are generally included within the course structure of a real estate school. Course work at this level is designed to cover the essentials of a very broad field. Practical experience and advanced courses (often taken in university programs) touch upon more advanced methods of selling, negotiating, networking, and the theories behind real estate strategies.

Your Licensing Exam

To obtain your real estate sales license, you need to meet the requirements of the state in which you will be selling real estate. The school at which you take your course work or the real estate license commission in your state can inform you of the specific licensing requirements.

You should check on such requirements prior to attending a school, and then again closer to the time when you plan to take the exam, because the laws may change in your state. The prerequisites for obtaining a license may also change. Typically, along with age requirements, completion of the course work at a recognized institution, and having a high school diploma (or GED equivalent), you may need to reside in the state in which you chose to be licensed and have a clean criminal record before you can take the exam. In addition, you will probably be asked to present the signed affidavit from the broker sponsoring you. In some states, you may also be required to work under the guidance of a licensed broker for one to two years after obtaining your license.

As for the exam itself, you will usually find questions on laws that affect the sale of property, mathmatic computations common to real estate practices, obligations and ethics of real estate transactions, and other material based on your coursework. Although formats change, and states may vary in the type of test they offer, real estate exams are generally multiple-choice tests. Some states give the exams in two parts, whereas others give a single exam on the various subject areas. You should ask an instructor which format will be used and how much time you will have to complete the test. You might also consider taking a preparatory course just prior to taking the exam. Private schools, community colleges, and online preparatory courses are widely available, as well as additional courses offered by the school you attended. Such additional courses can help you prepare for your licensing exam and also provide additional education. For example, one online school offers the following courses:

- Finance I
- Marketing: Building a Real Estate Practice
- Principles of Real Estate
- Real Estate Ethics and Professional Conduct: NAR Mandatory Ethics Training
- Real Estate Finance
- Tax Favorable Real Estate Transactions

The state licensing agency can provide you with details as to when and where the exam is given and what you can bring with you. Typically calculators (quiet ones that are nonprogrammable) are permitted and necessary. Hint: Make sure you have fresh batteries! You also receive an entry permit when you sign up to take the test. Bring this with you. The paperwork and time in which it must be completed will differ from state to state. You will then either receive an entry permit or your name will be put into a data base prior to taking the exam. Typically, you need pencils, a pen, and a photo ID. You may also need to show your certificate of completion from the course you have taken. If you are not sure what your state requires, contact the licensing bureau and ask. Also, don't panic if you do not do well on the exam. States usually allow candidates to take the exam more than once.

Ongoing Training

Real estate licenses in most states last for two years and are then renewable by completing continuing education requirements as mandated by the individual state, generally three or four courses, or 10 to 15 hours of course work. The same schools that provide initial training usually offer the post-licensing courses needed to maintain a license. Of course, you can also take such real estate courses at any accredited school that offers them. Many real estate agents today combine in-class hours with online courses to fulfill their continuing education requirements. Make sure to check that the courses you choose will be accepted for fulfilling the license renewal requirements.

Continuing education courses often focus on the changing face of the real estate industry, covering topics such as legislative updates and new real estate laws. Other courses may focus on real estate taxes, environmental issues, pricing properties to sell in the current market, maintaining professional ethics and standards, risk management, and how to handle offers and counter offers. Certain core requirements may be designated by the state licensing commission. If not, you can select the courses of interest to you.

As long as you complete the work prior to the expiration date of your license, you can renew your real estate license.

Finding the Right Real Estate Firm for You

Most new agents will seek a firm in their immediate area or an area in which they have previously resided. Doing so allows you to utilize your existing knowledge of the area. Remember, part of selling a home, office, or retail location is selling the neighborhood.

First and foremost, you want to work in a professional setting. Whether you choose a large firm or a small office with five or six people, you want to be part of a firm that is respected in the community.

To start your hunt, you should look at local real estate listings and make a list of potential firms. Take note of the For Sale signs you see in your neighborhood. Firms that have a lot of signs up are certainly active in your area and worth checking out. Some firms will be local offices of major franchises such as Century 21, whereas others will be small mom-and-pop-owned and run firms. In fact, in many areas you'll find a range of options. When calling the smaller firms, you may reach the broker directly; larger firms may put you in touch with the broker or have you first meet a recruitment officer or the office manager. Either way, your goal is to set up a meeting to discuss working at the firm as an agent.

Before contacting the firms on your list, you might want to contact the local chamber of commerce to gather some background information. In addition, you should network locally to see if you can learn more about the real estate firms in your area. Talk to local realtors and see what they have to say about their firms. Keep in mind, however, that opinions will vary, and you need to separate fact from gossip.

Prior to contacting real estate firms, you should consider whether a small or large firm would be better for your needs. Typically, larger firms offer more extensive training programs for new agents, have a greater presence in the neighborhoods where they do business, and can do more advertising and promotion. In fact, they may give you your own web page. In addition, some large firms are hooked up with nationwide networks for relocation. However, large firms have more agents, meaning you will be one among many agents on the schedule for phone duty, and there will be greater competition when it comes to picking up leads. There will also be more policies that you will need to adhere to and protocol to follow.

A small firm may provide you with more hands-on experience, as you will be expected to take on greater responsibilities, thus learning more as you go. As one of only a few agents, you will have greater access to leads, less competition, and fewer policies and regulations to follow. However, small firms need to work harder to establish a presence in a neighborhood. Limited resources on the part of a small firm may mean that you are expected to spend more of your own money on advertising and for other types of marketing and/or promotion.

In short, when weighing the options and deciding between a large or small firm, it usually becomes the familiar small fish in a big pond versus big fish in a small pond scenario. Which would you rather be? Ask yourself:

- Am I comfortable with the potential competition at a large firm?
- Can I handle various roles and responsibilities that may be thrust upon me at a small firm?
- If necessary, can I afford to lay our more of my own money at a smaller firm?

Many people get their feet wet at smaller firms before joining bigger firms. Conversely, some people leave a larger firm to essentially run a small firm—typically getting their brokers license along the way.

Interviewing with Real Estate Firms

Unlike the more traditional job interview, you may find the interview with a broker, recruitment officer, or office manager to be more of a two-way street. This is because while you are working at the firm, you are also carving your own niche. You are not an "employee" in the traditional sense, receiving payment for doing a job, but instead you are serving as an independent contractor handling your own business within the structure of a firm. Speaking up clearly and showing your ability to communicate well is advantageous in an industry that focuses heavily on good communication skills. Demonstrating your real estate skills and displaying your "real estate personality" can also impress a broker or recruitment manager.

It is important to find out more about how the agency works. For example, find out how floor duty, phone time, or "opportunity hours" (as they are sometimes called) are handled. Do you have regular hours every week when you answer phones, or is it a flexible schedule? How are leads distributed when you are on floor duty and at other times? Do you contribute to advertising costs? Will you need to join certain associations or become part of any organizations? What are the commissions for sales? Are they paid on a sliding scale that increases as you bring in larger deals or as you earn seniority? Are you responsible for your own office supplies and/or equipment? Many of these answers will be provided as part of the information given by the broker or recruitment manager.

Overall, the three biggest areas of concern are typically

1. the manner in which you are able to gather leads and build up your database;
2. how much you can make in commissions;
3. what expenses you are expected to pay.

As a beginner, you will be seen as the new kid in town. Therefore, you will not be privy to as many leads as the senior agents and your initial commissions will likely be lower. In addition, you will very likely be spending more money than you are making in the beginning. The big question is how and when will that change? This is what you really want to learn in the interview. There's nothing wrong with paying your dues, which you will do literally as well as figuratively. Training will likely prove to be very valuable. However, you need to understand how the system is designed to work once you have been there a while. Can you see a bright future after paying your dues?

Also, while at a real estate firm, you can get a feel for the overall atmosphere. Is there an atmosphere of cooperation and community? Do the agents appear to be enjoying their work? Is the atmosphere cold and sterile? You will also want to find out if agents come and go frequently. If there is a high turnover rate, that may be a strong indicator that something is not quite right about either the way the firm is operating or the atmosphere. Atmosphere in which you work makes a difference in productivity, and while eventually you won't spend as much time in the office as in the field, you want to be at a place where you can feel good about showing up at work every day.

Spending Money to Make Money

One of the advantages of a real estate career is that by having a license to sell and being an independent contractor, you have more freedom than in other professions. Within the brokerage firm, you can get valuable training, establish yourself as an agent, and build up your own database, while having the freedom to work on a flexible schedule. However, there is a price for such freedom. In the first year, expenses can overshadow income, so you need to be sure as you move into your real estate career that you have enough savings or income from another source while you are getting started. Some expenses continue throughout your real estate career, whereas others are part of getting started. Typical expenses include:

- Real estate prelicensing school
- Books and other materials for school
- Licensing preparatory course
- Licensing exam
- Business licenses—depending on the state
- Business cards
- Multiple listing service fees
- Fees to join real estate boards
- Fees to join other local associations and dues to remain a member
- Possible training fees, depending on the firm
- Errors and omissions insurance coverage
- Your own web site
- Continuing education courses
- Advertising
- Business expenses, which can include phone calls, copies, postage, letterhead stationery, business cards, and various other office supplies
- Software programs and/or technical expenses
- Auto related expenses, including gas and repairs
- Liability insurance

Clearly there will be some cash layout in order to get started plus ongoing expenses as you proceed in your career. You should keep an ongoing record, or daily log, of all such expenses. On a positive note, you will have plenty of business expenses to claim as deductions on your tax return. Hint: Save your receipts!

On-the-Job Training

As is the usually case when learning a profession, there is a gap between the education you receive from courses and those that you receive from real-world training and experience. In the case of real estate, this may be a wider gap because the education process is fairly short, and responsibilities encompass so much detail.

You can, and will, learn a lot by simply working in a real estate office. Sometimes, people interested in careers in real estate take administrative jobs simply to get an idea of some of the basics. For example, you can learn how to deal effectively with prospective clients on the phone, answer client questions, and get an understanding of what does and does not go into a standard contract by working in a real estate office in a supportive capacity while taking your pre-exam courses. This way you are learning on the job, possibly even as an intern.

If you are fortunate enough to find a mentor, be observant and see how he handles the wide range of unique situations that can occur during a real estate transaction. Besides learning the seemingly endless array of details, from disclaimers to closing documents, you want to learn how to confidently guide clients through all sorts of potential concerns that they may have during the selling or buying process.

In addition to learning at the office and from more experienced sales agents, you can learn a lot by reading real estate magazines and books, looking at web sites, joining local associations and/or organizations, and even reading your office manual carefully. You can also seek out seminars on improving sales techniques, lead generation, and other topics.

Additional Training and Special Skills to Enhance Your Career

If you are serious about moving ahead of the competition and starting to make a name for yourself as an agent, you may consider going to school to obtain additional training in the field, or in related fields. Numerous colleges are now offering real estate courses and degrees. An associate degree program in real estate typically includes courses in a wide range of subjects including:

- Communications
- Principles of economics
- Computer applications in business
- Accounting
- Real estate practices
- Principles of management and organization
- Real estate finance
- Real estate appraisal
- Real estate law
- Sales techniques

Many major universities also offer real estate degrees. A few of the schools offering such degrees are:

- Arizona Real Estate Center
- California State University—LA Real Estate Program
- Cornell University—Program in Real Estate
- Florida State University Real Estate Research Center
- Georgia State University Real Estate Research Center
- Indiana University Center for Real Estate
- Institute for Real Estate Studies, Pennsylvania State University
- Joint Center for Housing Studies of Harvard University
- New York University Real Estate Institute
- Ohio State University for Real Estate Education and Research
- Oxford Centre for Real Estate Management
- UC Berkeley Center for Real Estate and Urban Economics
- University of Cincinnati Real Estate Program
- University of Colorado Real Estate Center
- University of Connecticut Center for Real Estate and Urban Economic Studies
- University of Georgia, Terry College of Business
- University of Southern Maine, Center for Real Estate Education
- Washington Center for Real Estate Research
- Virginia Center for Housing Research

While having a degree can enhance your status and improve your commissions, learning about appraisals, having a greater knowledge of construction, understanding the inspection process, and/or learning more about architecture can also prove helpful in your real estate career. Whether or not you plan to go for your broker's license, become an office manager, or move into another real estate related career, the additional knowledge can make you a sought after salesperson. It can also help you when evaluating properties to list or for buyers. One of the most intriguing aspects of real estate is that because it incorporates so many areas of expertise, you may find yourself learning about something of personal interest that can also help your career. For example, landscaping or gardening can be useful skills when selling residential properties. Home decorating courses can also prove beneficial. If you have an interest in technology, you may be first in line to utilize new software programs and may end up in a position to train other agents in how to use the new technology.

If you are serious about gaining the proverbial "competitive edge" in a highly competitive field, you may find an area of interest that becomes your niche or specialty in the field, thus making you an expert in that area and resulting in higher commissions.

In the next chapter, there is more discussion of other careers you can move into once you have made the initial

foray into real estate. In the meantime, Figure 3.1 is a good example of the type of questions you will find on real estate licensing exams.

FIGURE 3.1

Sample Real Estate Licensing Exam Questions

Below are questions similar to those you see on licensing exams in most states. It is always recommended that you read through each question carefully and answer those you feel you know first before going back to the more difficult questions in which you have less confidence that you know the answer. For those questions that you are not sure about, try to narrow your answer down to the best two possibilities before making a choice.

1. An exclusive-right-to-lease agreement must include specific information. Which of the following is not required in such a contract?

   a. The lease price

   b. An automatic lease renewal clause

   c. Commission expected on the lease

   d. The duration of the lease agreement

2. A buyer gives a salesperson a check for escrow money. At that time, which of the following is necessary?

   a. The salesperson must immediately deposit the check in the broker's escrow account.

   b. The salesperson must deposit the check in the seller's bank account.

   c. The salesperson has until the end of the next business day to deposit the check in the broker's escrow account.

   d. The salesperson must open an escrow account in his or her name and deposit the check.

3. The Real Estate Commission has the authority to:

   a. Appoint commissioners

   b. Conduct licensing examinations

   c. Run affiliated real estate schools

   d. Promulgate rules and regulations

4. Mr. and Mrs. James contacted and met with real estate agent A, who showed them several houses in a specific neighborhood. Two months later they were shown a house they had not yet seen in the same neighborhood by real estate agent B, which they ended up purchasing. From this transaction, agent A should receive:

   a. A split brokers fee

   b. A partial commission from agent B

c. A partial commission if the home was also on agent A's listing of houses from the MLS.

d. Nothing, unless there was a signed buyers agreement

5. Mr. Brown is purchasing a condo unit and obtaining financing from a local bank. In this situation, which best describes Mr. Brown?

a. A leasor

b. A vendor

c. A mortgagor

d. A seller

6. When a broker receives a check from a buyer and deposits it in an escrow account, that is to protect him or her against a potential charge of:

a. Commingling

b. Embezzlement

c. Novation

d. Losing the funds

7. A loan originated in a bank may be sold in the:

a. Primary market

b. Secondary market

c. Mortgage market

d. REITS market

These are just a few of the potential questions you could see on your licensing exam. If some of them are confusing now, don't worry, after your course work they should be much easier to answer.

In case you are wondering, the answers are:

1:b, 2:c, 3:d, 4:d, 5:c, 6:a, 7:b

■   ■   ■

CHAPTER 4

Beyond an Agent
Other Real Estate
Career Options

knows her surrounding neighborhoods inside and out. "I've raised my kids here," she adds, referring to her four children, who have given the 60-plus-year-old former teacher's assistant and ex-city counsel member nine grandchildren. Knowing the area helps her pinpoint the demographic groups that she wants to reach with her marketing efforts.

Under the watchful eye of Falcone, many young real estate agents have blossomed at the White Plains office, during her 18-year tenure. "I recommend that the new agents take every class offered because with each class you gain knowledge," notes Falcone. "Agents must treat this as a business and spend money to make money," she adds, referring to promoting themselves and making their presence known, something that comes easily to the outgoing office manager who has a tremendous zest for life. Falcone still enjoys skiing, riding a wave runner, and even bungee jumping, which she and her husband (also named Joe) did to celebrate their 35th wedding anniversary.

■ ■ ■

It is estimated that about five million people work in some aspect of real estate, and the most common job is real estate agent. But the industry could not run with only agents. Real estate brokers, commercial agents and brokers, office managers, property managers, developers, appraisers, planners, mortgage brokers, and researchers all play a vital role. By launching your career as a real estate agent, you can gain the basic skills, knowledge, and experience in the field that carries over into these related jobs. This job is also the most logical starting point because you can become an agent in a relatively short time, and because being an agent gives you an opportunity to use a wide range of skills.

One of the necessary skills for any position in the real estate industry is a good aptitude for numbers. From pricing to square footage to acreage, your ability to understand formulas and computations will be tested in most areas of real estate. Calculators can provide the final computations, but you need to know what you are doing. The ability to research and understand legal terminology as it pertains to property and landholdings is also a valuable skill. To master abilities such as these, you need to exercise patience, be detail oriented, and be good at follow-through.

One of the most appealing aspects of many real estate careers is that they are self-managed, meaning you have some freedom and flexibility to set a pace that meets your needs and lifestyle. The majority of real estate professionals are independent contractors who are able to select the area and environment where they feel comfortable working.

Real Estate Broker

While those outside the industry use the terms *broker* and *agent* interchangeably, there is a significant difference. Unlike agents, brokers are able to open up real estate offices and place listings. They may then take responsibility for sponsoring and hiring real estate agents. Brokers in most states need additional education and training beyond that of agents and are required to take a separate licensing exam. Typically, brokers are required to have worked previously as agents.

Because brokers open real estate offices, they are responsible for the listings as well as advertisements placed by that office. Brokers will often use their advanced training and experience to work with and train newer agents. In addition, brokers are more closely involved in arranging financing for prospective buyers, and they have fiduciary responsibility for the actions of their agents. Management, organizational, administrative, and technical skills are necessary to handle this position, as are strong communication skills and the ability to judge talent when bringing new agents onboard.

Commercial Agents and Brokers

There are far fewer agents and brokers in commercial real estate, but there is a lot of money to be made here. Agents and brokers have a working relationship similar to that in residential real estate: Brokers own and manage commercial real estate offices, and sales agents make the actual deals. Beyond that, commercial brokerage is a whole new ballgame. Both deals and offices can be very big—and complex. There are whole new sets of laws and regulations.

Commercial agents and brokers specialize in income-producing properties: retail stores, shopping centers, office buildings, warehouses, manufacturing centers, office parks, hotels, and apartment buildings. Commercial brokers and agents representing the buyers or sellers are selling/buying the physical property and the growth potential of the business. Although the sale of a commercial property is similar to the sale of a home in principle—getting a good price for the seller—the price is based not only on the actual property but also on the potential for the new property owner to make money. For buyers, numerous factors enter into the equation when trying to determine whether or not the business can thrive in a specific location.

To do this job effectively, commercial brokers and agents need to be familiar with market analysis, the potential for growth and income, negotiations, business tax laws and regulations, zoning restrictions, and other factors that may limit or enhance the success of the business. In addition, leases are more complex. For example, some leases include clauses that do not allow competitive businesses to open in a close proximity, and others allow a small growing business to sublease their unused space.

Besides a knack for sales, there is also a need to understand the many factors involved in making the right investment decisions because commercial real estate buyers are looking for a good return on their investments. Therefore, you can find yourself analyzing financial data and the valuation placed on a property, including areas such as inventory, receivables, or intellectual properties that may be part of the sale. You need to know what *location, location, location* really means, why a location is or is not viable for a buyer, or whether a seller is asking too much for a struggling business.

Understanding the needs of a business will ultimately be the key to your success. Can you help a client find an office suite in a mixed-use development with potential for growth? Can you help a retail storeowner find a prime location in a shopping mall? Can you help a small business owner determine a value and sell his business in a down market by providing seller-finance to help the buyer meet the asking price? There are numerous scenarios, and most commercial agents and brokers spend more time crunching numbers than do those agents and brokers who are selling homes.

Because there are so many potential areas under the heading "commercial real estate," most brokers and agents specialize. For example, you may elect to specialize in suburban office parks, industrial properties, hotels and motels, shopping centers, or golf courses. By specializing, you limit the number of clients you can take on, but you can gain a strong reputation in an area and become a leading player in that field. Generally, in commercial real estate it is recommended that you excel in one (or a few) areas, rather than trying to be a jack-of-all-trades. Major commercial real estate firms typically offer various services, so you can be hired to handle your specialty for that firm.

Unlike residential real estate, the hours in commercial real estate are often less flexible, and there is a lot more in-office work to be done. You may find yourself involved in multimillion dollar deals and need to have a wealth of information available at your fingertips. Technical knowledge is a must in commercial real estate, along with a well-honed business persona, and strong business ethics. The potential for major deals is more common, and therefore, commercial real estate has less "handholding" and more "corporate" business dealings.

Keep in mind, however, that because of the details, complexities, and need for businesses to obtain funding, it can take longer to get that first deal than in residential real estate—and that can often be many months.

Real Estate Office Manager

The real estate office manager, typically a broker, has the job of positioning the real estate firm for success in a competitive arena. Strategic planning to gain a market share in the community is vital. Office managers usually have significant experience in the field and understand the needs of sales agents and research assistants. Whereas sales agents typically work as independent contractors, managers adhere to a more traditional work schedule and spend far more time in the office handling the responsibilities that go along with running a business.

Some real estate office managers climb the ladder from within, taking over for the existing manager when she retires or moves to another location. However, you may choose to take management courses and apply to a large real estate company in hopes of managing one of its offices. In this case, you will probably start out with a smaller office or one that has not been as profitable, meaning you will have the job of righting the ship.

As a new office manager, your job is to assess current conditions and determine what needs to be done to increase sales, which may include anything from upgrading the actual facility by bringing in new technology to a paint/decorating job to entice new customers to stay a while. You need to study the business operations from previous years, review the success of the sales agents, assess the neighborhood and the local real estate climate, look over the expense reports, and determine what it will take to build the office into a successful venture.

To succeed as an office manager, your management tools should include good communications skills as well as attention to detail and strong follow-through. You need to have an understanding of what makes an office function in a productive manner, how to hire agents, and how to delegate responsibilities to support staff. Long hours and great responsibility always rest on the shoulders of management. It can pay off handsomely if you have a thriving real estate office.

Property Manager

Property managers are in charge of maintaining and overseeing real estate properties. They are paid well to make sure a property continues to produce strong financial returns consistently over a long period of time. In short, they protect the investments of the owners.

Frequently property managers handle several properties at one time. If these are residential properties, they could include apartment developments, individual apartment buildings, condominiums, and/or retirement communities. Commercial property managers oversee office buildings, shopping centers, hotels, and/or individual retail outlets under the same ownership. Property managers may work for large real estate firms, banks, investment companies, and/or trust companies in the real estate division. They can also work for private companies that own real estate.

The job combines business abilities with interpersonal skills. Negotiating leases and determining how to make the most potential profit from space allocation is part of the business end of the job. Dealing with tenants, collecting rent, and working with contractors, builders, vendors, repair and maintenance engineers, and anyone else involved in the maintenance and upkeep of the property utilizes interpersonal skills. It is also important to be able to find practical, logical, and ethical solutions to a wide range of problems that occur within a property. From tenant complaints to union work stoppages, the often round-the-clock job can certainly have many trying moments. Being patient and keeping a clear head when all is not going well is an important attribute.

Land Broker and Developer

Land brokers primarily buy and sell land for the purposes of housing, commercial use, and farming. However, the key to succeeding as a land broker is being able to evaluate the land and produce feasibility studies that demonstrate the potential use for generating income from that land. Developing land to be better suited for a potential use is also part of the process and entails knowing the factors involved in determining the value of a piece of land. For example, is the land suitable for farming? Can the land, at present, support a structure? What size? From a high-rise apartment building to a sprawling golf course, land is at the basis of real estate, and it needs to be utilized appropriately.

Land development also may include overseeing the formation of infrastructure, and such a developer may be involved in the entire process from bidding to construction. A good land broker and/or developer can create a situation whereby the land sells for top value and is profitable for the owner.

You need to have a keen understanding of the valuation of land, strong math and economic skills, an ability to sell, good communication skills, and enjoy working outdoors before venturing into this high paying but very specialized area of real estate.

Real Estate Appraiser

Real estate appraisers determine the value of properties, including homes, commercial buildings, tracts of land, or combinations. There are several values determined through the work of an appraiser, including investment value, assessed value for tax purposes, insurance value, and/or rental value. Values placed on a property by an appraiser weigh heavily on any potential transaction. They also influence the mortgage a lender will offer. Therefore, appraisers need to be carefully trained and have a thorough knowledge and understanding of the principles of appraising a property. A technical education, math skills, some accounting knowledge, and strong business ethics are all part of this job.

Like agents and brokers, appraisers must be 18 years or older and high school graduates, or have a GED high school equivalent diploma. To get started, you must attend classes recognized by the appraisal board in your state. Upon completion of your classes, which may include final exams depending on the school and state requirements, you are entitled to take an exam to become a licensed appraiser in your state. Some states have additional requirements such as experience in the real estate field before taking the exam or before practicing as a licensed appraiser.

Once you are licensed, your job as an appraiser will set you apart from affiliating professionally with any other real estate professionals. Appraisers must maintain their independence to be total unbiased while doing their jobs. The job of an appraiser can have significant impact upon a sale or purchase of real estate, upon the individuals, and even the community involved. Therefore, an appraiser must be prepared to use professional standards and practices to gather, analyze, and use all pertinent information in making the determination of a specific value. He must then be prepared to present the information to the client, who is often a lender or mortgage broker.

As an appraiser, you will evaluate the condition of the property, reviewing the inside and outside as well as the documentation of any additions, changes, or upgrades that have been made to the property. Square footage, building materials used, and other factors will determine your assessment. Typically, appraisers only focus on permanent aspects of the property and/or upon the actual land.

If you have a very good eye for detail, a fact-finding personality, practical, analytical, meticulous habits, and an unwavering work ethic, you might consider this real estate career.

Urban Planner

Do you enjoy those television shows where somebody comes in and does a complete makeover of a home or apartment? If you do, then urban planning might be in your future. Urban planners develop and work on plans to revitalize and rejuvenate entire urban and suburban communities. Typically employed by local governments, urban planners (also called regional or city planners) team with government officials to review the socioeconomic conditions of neighborhoods and determine what they can do to make significant improvements. From traffic and parking considerations, to neighborhood parks, to recreational facilities, schools, and public transportation and environmental concerns, the job entails doing a complete "makeover" of a neighborhood.

Although a very time-consuming profession, an urban planner can take great pride in, and make good money in this profession. You need to be able to multitask (in a big way), be a very good problem solver, and have great attention for detail. Good communication skills are very important because you will be working with engineers, architects, politicians, civic and local leaders, tenant boards, environmentalists, inspectors, and potentially anyone else who wants to have a say in the future of the community. Economic skills are necessary because you will do reports that include the financial and budgetary plans for all of your proposed projects. Technical skills also heavily factor into the life of the modern urban planner. Computerized geographic information systems allow such planners to overlay maps with geographic variables, such as population density, and to combine or manipulate geographic information to produce various plans for the development of the land.

Among the many skills necessary for such a position, public speaking is critical. In order to generate support and sometimes out of a need to defend your plan, you will find yourself speaking in front of neighborhood groups, civic leaders, and even local politicians. Typically, you will need a masters degree in urban or regional planning to become an urban or regional planner. Accreditation for the masters programs at various universities comes from the Planning Accreditation Board, which consists of representatives of the American Institute of Certified Planners, the American Planning Association, and the Association of Collegiate Schools of Planning.

Mortgage Broker

Unlike many of the other careers in real estate, this is a desk job. It is, however, a significant career option, because mortgage lenders play a major role in real estate transactions. The mortgage broker connects lenders with borrowers. The reason borrowers go to mortgage brokers rather than directly to lenders is because they can offer borrowers far more loans—otherwise they would have to go from lender to lender, which is time consuming and a danger to their credit rating (due to numerous requests for a credit report).

As a mortgage broker, you will need to be knowledgeable about the lending market on a daily basis and know the loan rates. You will be offering the loan products of various lenders, known as wholesalers, to your clients, and depending on their needs, advising them accordingly. There is a significant amount of paperwork involved because you will be putting together files on prospective borrowers, which will include their credit reports. You will then approach the lenders, who will determine whether the borrower is a safe risk or not.

You can mark up the rates that you receive from the wholesaler. This is where you receive your payment. For example, if a lender has a loan product at 6.5 percent with no points, you can add 1 point, which is the same as 1 percent of the loan. You make your money from that point. You collect your 1 percent at the time of the closing. In a highly competitive real estate market, you need to judge accordingly how much you can or cannot mark up a mortgage. If you are savvy, you can set the loan as high as you like and go for more money. However, if the prospective borrowers are also savvy, they can shop around and go with another broker who beats your price. Therefore, it's a job that involves not only strong math skills and an economics background, but also some poker skills.

Salesmanship, strong people skills, and good number skills are all necessary in this position. You will need to be comfortable working with real estate agents, brokers, buyers, attorneys, and, of course, the many lenders you represent.

Researcher

Brokers, property managers, agents, appraisers, and other real estate professionals all require research. As a researcher, you can gain valuable knowledge and experience in the industry.

From housing and building records, to personal files kept on customers, to industry trends and financial data, there are millions of recorded documents in real estate. Companies like the CoStar Group specialize in real estate research. CoStar has 700 highly-skilled researchers trained to locate anything you could want to know about a property.

Obviously, you need to enjoy tracking down information and/or searching the web if you are going to consider going into the research field. You need to be meticulous, detail oriented, and tenacious with a never-give-up attitude.

Top researchers take pride in their ability to pull seemingly hard-to-find data out of their hats. Some go on to head research departments in major firms.

Salaries

Real estate salaries run the gamut from $15,000 to over $1.2 million, depending where you are in your career and the properties with which you are involved. The middle 50 percent of full-time real estate agents, who earn a salary and commissions, generally earn between $23,000 and $54,000, with a median salary of about $32,000. Brokers, however, will earn more, with their median pay topping the $50,000 mark in 2002 and now near $54,000. Depending on the community and the state of the real estate industry, brokers' income ranges anywhere from $20,000 to $500,000, but more typically is in the $40,000 to $80,000 range.

Typically, commissions on a residential property range from 5 to 7 percent and are slightly higher for commercial properties. Raw land commissions are usually around 10 percent. The range of commissions depends on the experience of the agent or broker, type of property, value of the property, structure of the deal, and the manner in which the firm sets up its commission schedule. Economic conditions also play a part in commissions. Because sales are not usually consistent from month to month, earnings for agents and brokers usually vary.

Office managers in brokerage firms typically earn between $60,000 and $90,000. Property managers' salaries are harder to pinpoint because they will vary depending on the number of properties and the types of properties being managed. Residential property managers may earn around $65,000, whereas a property manager for a large shopping mall may earn $80,000. The median salary for the property manager for an office building is about $100,000.

Appraisers for commercial real estate can expect to earn between $70,000 and $80,000; those who handle residential real estate will earn in the $35,000 to $40,000 range.

The median annual earnings of urban and regional planners is just over $50,000, with the middle 50 percent in the $40,000 to $65,000 range. It is a growing field, however, and as more planners are needed, the salaries may go up.

As for the top corporate real estate executives, the average pay has topped $230,000, and the sky is the limit.

What You
Need to Know

For Sandra Lippman, learning what she needed to know about real estate was in part thanks to the broker at the Prudential Centennial of Scarsdale, New York, where Sandra is a licensed sales agent. "He gives a lot of training, which is very helpful, especially with all the forms and paperwork that are required in real estate."

A native of Westchester County, Lippman took up real estate in 1998, following a career as a speech pathologist in the New York

City school system and a communications teacher for two universities. While looking for something new, she met with a friend who told her how much she loved her job. "People don't say that very often," says Lippman, whose friend was selling real estate. "Since I was always taking some type of course, I thought I'd take a real estate course and see if I liked it," she adds.

Now, some eight years into the field, although she now has a firm grasp of the business, it took some on-the-job learning. "I remember when I started out, I showed a 'prospective' buyer 57 houses and they ended up renting a place through someone else," says Lippman. "However, it was a helpful experience because I learned my way around areas of the county that I didn't know very well," she adds, taking the positive approach. "You learn a lot while you are doing the job," explains Lippman, who also notes that now she can usually tell very quickly if a buyer is or is not "serious."

Not having a large sphere of influence when she started in the field, Lippman decided to post her own web site in 1998 when the internet was still gaining steam. Today, she continues to work hard at maintaining the site, well aware that it has helped her tremendously. Sandra also recognizes the value of having a background in communications. "In this field you need to be able to talk to people, and you must get back to people quickly. If you get a message and let it sit for a week, you'll lose that customer's business," says

Lippman, who is quick to respond to callers and to anyone who e-mails her after visiting her web site at www.sandyfor realestate.com.

■   ■   ■

Every industry has a significant amount of industry-specific information, and real estate is no exception. In fact, real estate has enough material for two or three industries. For that reason, agents and brokers are constantly learning and referring to specialists in the field, such as real estate attorneys or consultants.

In this section, you'll take a look at some of the basics, including the tangibles such as reports you can analyze, and some intangibles such as the theories behind the buying and selling of property. Your job in real estate can have a significant impact on clients, whether they are selling properties, buying homes for their families, leasing corporate office facilities for their companies, or seeking the best retail locations for their stores.

Selling Homes, Not Just Houses

A house is a structure, while a home is a place where people share their dreams, hopes, and goals, make decisions—some good, some bad—share their thoughts, raise children, experience pleasure and pain, and create memories. It is easy to sell a house to a rich investor who simply looks at it as an asset. You need only know the value of the house and the projected return on the investment in the coming years. Then it becomes a business deal.

Selling homes, however, is a bit more complicated. It entails meeting the needs of both buyers and sellers. You want to get the best deal for a seller but also understand the need to sell: How fast they want, or need, to move. For a buyer, you need to see beyond the basic parameters and get a sense of what it is that makes her tick. A home for a young married couple and a home for empty nesters may be the same in the number of rooms and square footage, but their needs, goals, and plans are likely to be different. For example, one room can be a library that will become the baby's room for the young couple, while the empty nesters may run a homebased business and need a home office. Same room, same house, different needs. As a real estate agent, you will learn to visualize how the rooms will best suit your buyers. You will learn to envision your buyers in a home or understand why your sellers are selling and what their needs are.

Representing Sellers

Typically, sellers have one primary focus—getting good prices for their properties. For this reason, they hire real estate agents (like yourself) and sign listing agreements.

The listing agreement is a contract between the seller (you), the agent, saying that you will list their property for a specified time, make an effort to sell the property, and receive a commission for doing so. Along with the term of the listing agreement, the listing price will be included.

However, selling a property and getting the asking price does not happen based on the "ask and you shall receive" principle. Therefore, before listing a property, or even agreeing to list it, you will want to carefully assess the property. If there appear to be significant problems with structure, wiring, or plumbing, you may want to have an inspector come in and file a report so that you have a better idea of the condition of the property. In the case of minor problems, the seller can probably make corrections and repairs. However, you will need to make notes and have as detailed a report on the property as possible before you decide to list it. Full disclosure is imperative on the part of the seller. It will save you both a lot of headaches. Even if you are not going to use them until after an offer has been made, have the seller sign a few disclosure forms so you will be prepared.

Keep in mind that full disclosure will also include the grounds around the house. The entire property is part of the sale, therefore anything the seller knows about the property needs to be disclosed. Additionally, make sure you know the boundaries of the property. If there are any disputes or concerns regarding the boundaries, you need to know about these and possibly do a title search. If additions were made to the house, you will want to make sure they were done legally and permits were issued. Cover all of your bases before you

STAGING

There are some real estate agents and brokers, who put on "stagings," that is, where they hire a team to turn the house into something off the set of HGTV. However, it is typically not something a seller wants to be a part of and most buyers today can see the mirrors through the smoke.

agree to try to sell a house and have buyers, or their agents, asking questions that you cannot answer. Remember, if there are problems, and buyers are not pleased with the answers, the house will not sell and your listing will expire. Therefore, address all possible issues in advance, so that if you do place a listing on the MLS, it will sell.

Therefore, your job as a representative for the seller is to set a price in accordance with what you determine the market dictates (based on your comparative analysis) and what you believe you can get for the property based on the number of homes currently on the market. Naturally you will aim high. In some markets, houses sell at or above listing prices, while in other markets homes generally are bargained down. By knowing the market and the property, you will be able to determine an asking price with your seller.

Then, once you are confident that no "hidden surprises" will turn up regarding the property, you will have the listing agreement signed, list the property on MLS, possibly hold an open house, advertise, and market your property.

If you have a buyer interested, you will present the offer to the seller. If the seller accepts the offer, you will start working on the many particulars that go into the final sale with the agent representing the buyer. You are representing the seller in the negotiation process. Typically, there will be several contingencies, such as the house passing an inspection. The seller may also be asked to pay for certain repairs or fees. Different regions have their own common practices. You will need to know what is customary in your area. Advise your client based on what is considered standard practice. If the buyer is making unreasonable demands, and you cannot compromise, you can advise your seller to wait for a better offer. Once an offer is accepted and contingencies are satisfied, you can start working with the seller toward the closing.

Representing Buyers

On the other side of the equation, you may find yourself representing buyers and showing them properties. You will first need to tour properties that become available in the area and then seek out the houses that fit the needs of your prospective buyers based on those that you have seen and those that appear on MLS. Remember, think about the home as a place where your buyers will be living and not strictly in terms of square feet and two-and-a-half baths. If you can't see the family or couple living in that house, chances are they can't either. Of course, you will need to determine who your clients are and what is important to them. You'd be amazed at how much people differ in what is important to them when house hunting. One person will fall in love with a brick fireplace, while another will need a large eat-in kitchen and still another must have a finished basement where the kids can go and play. To each their own. However, you can only sell them on what is there. Again, listen carefully and try to accentuate the positives that THEY are looking for . . . if they exist. *No, you can't run downstairs and build a fireplace while they are upstairs!*

From a practical standpoint, you need to make sure your buyers are pre-approved for a mortgage loan so that they can make an offer and have it taken seriously. Therefore, if they are not pre-approved, encourage serious clients to get that taken care of.

You then need to learn the basic information about each buyer. Have they ever purchased a home before or are they first-time homebuyers? If they own a home, is it already on the market or are they planning to put it on the market soon? What price range are they considering, and how much of that can they put down as a down payment? What is the makeup of the family? What are they looking for in a home?

First-time buyers, more so then sellers, need to be talked through the transaction process. Sellers have generally been involved in a real estate transaction at least once before . . . buying the home they are now selling. For buyers, you will need to stay on top of the listings. In some areas you will need to act fast, as homes sell very quickly. You'll get to know the selling pace of the neighborhood in which you are working. In the course of representing buyers and sellers you will have occasion to refer them to other professionals, such as an inspector or a contractor. One of the personal requirements of being a good sales agent is to have your contacts established early on in your career. You want to be ready to call on, or refer clients to, good people, so get to know some quality inspectors before you start working with clients.

Many real estate agents say they enjoy driving potential buyers around and showing them homes; just remember that you need to see the homes in advance. Also, always use your own car to show homes to prospective buyers. Although most states have no contracts between agents and prospective buyers, there are some that have buyer agreements. In this case, once you establish a relationship with a client, you have them sign that they will work exclusively with you to find and purchase a home for a specific time period.

If buyers want to make an offer, you will need to sit down at your office and go over the process of making an offer. If the buyers are certain that they want to proceed, then you will present their offer and wait for a response.

If an offer is accepted, you will want to celebrate, but you shouldn't . . . at least not yet. There will typically be contingencies, such as a home inspection and the loan approval. Pre-approval usually means the loan will be approved, but it's not a done deal until the lender formally approves it. Also, you will have the prospective buyers open an escrow account and get busy completing all of the paperwork as required in your state. You will work together with the seller's agent to put together the deal, and once everything has been ironed out, you will proceed through the closing with your buyers. Once you have completed the closing, typically a few months after the acceptance of the offer, and the closing documents are signed, sealed, and put in the files, you can celebrate.

Selling Businesses, Not Just Office or Retail Space

In commercial real estate, similar principles hold true. You are selling a place from which to build or grow a business, not just raw space.

In commercial real estate, the primary focus is on whether or not the space is conducive to the needs of a business enjoying success and growth. Minor repairs are typically less of an issue than if the facility meets the particular company's practical needs. You need to determine what the market rate is for a given space and guide the seller or landlord renting/leasing the property accordingly. Again, knowing what price range is typically acceptable in your region is very important. You also want to know what concessions sellers typically make in your area, and what standard leases in similar facilities include. Familiarize yourself with other leases and determine if your seller has enough added value to justify a higher price.

Just as you look at homes before showing them to clients, do the same with office space, retail facilities, warehouses, or industrial complexes. You also need to have experts at the ready, including engineers, to determine what is and is not feasible. For example, can the current wiring handle the technical needs of a high-tech company looking to move in?

The business mind-set requires that you see the bigger picture. Can the company turn a profit here? Depending on the type of business, you will probably need to consider some of the following:

- The need for a high traffic location. Some businesses need this, while others do not.
- The technical infrastructure of the facility
- The potential for growth: Can it rent or buy neighboring space if necessary?
- Parking or mass transit, depending on the region
- Access to major roads
- Loading docks
- Local zoning ordinances
- The physical appearance of the facility: For some business this will matter, whereas for others it will be irrelevant.
- Adequate storage space
- Restrooms and kitchen facilities
- Environmental concerns
- Safety and security concerns
- Structural concerns

There are many considerations that need to be addressed. You need to look at a business and take into account its concerns. For example, if a retail store relies on walk-in traffic, then location, location, location matters most. Conversely, for an internet business, the location of the company may not matter at all. The need for a large office space that can accommodate state-of-the art technical equipment will be more significant. You may represent a small growing company seeking a larger space than it needs right now, in order to allow for growth. In the meantime, the business owner may plan to make money by renting out the portion of the facility that it is not using.

There are many more details in commercial real estate than in residential real estate, but the bottom line is the same: The seller or landlord wants as much as he can get for the place while the buyer wants a space that meets the needs of her business.

Know Your Neighborhood

A million dollar home next to a polluted river is no longer a million dollar home—unless, perhaps, the buyer has a very poor sense of smell. The value of real estate is obviously dependant on where the real estate is located. In fact, the house in Westchester, New York, that sells for $800,000 could easily sell for $300,000 in Kansas. Although people want nice homes, and companies want facilities in which they can successfully conduct their business, the city, town, village, or hamlet in which a property is located is a primary factor in nearly all real estate deals.

Therefore, you are not only selling property, you are selling a neighborhood. The internet has been a godsend when it comes to finding neighborhood data. However, a word of caution—check the date of the posting carefully. Some web sites are updated often while others lag behind, sometimes by several years.

Among the information you want to look at, along with school and crime reports, are: The turnover rate of properties, local real estate taxes, zoning laws, high and low traffic areas, recreational opportunities, shopping locations, and the current overall market for housing and business. You not only need to have the pulse of the neighborhood, you also must be on top of upcoming changes to the infrastructure, pending construction, and other factors that could affect not only the value of the property you are representing, but also those in which buyers are interested.

Drive around, talk to store owners, homeowners, teachers, police officers, civic leaders, community leaders, and planners. Attend local meetings, read the local papers, and stay abreast of what is taking place. If you are already living in the area, you'll have a heads up, but don't think that by virtue of living there you know it all. Do a little research. You'll be surprised at all that you can learn.

Appraisals

You need to know the appraisal value of the property you are selling or looking at with buyers. The appraised value of a property is based on a variety of factors, including the size and condition of the property, the materials used in the construction, and the various amenities, or additions, to the structure. Recent area sales are also taken into consideration because they present a basis for comparison. You should use the appraisal value as a guideline when setting the price for a home or assisting buyers when bidding on the property.

Deeds, Titles, Permits, and other Documents

The deed is the legal document that transfers legal ownership of the property from one owner to another. The title is the legal document that indicates ownership of the property. You will become familiar with both of these terms in your real estate courses. A title search comes up as part of the closing process to make sure that the property is rightfully owned by the seller.

Building permits are essentially documents that provide a property owner local government permission to construct, repair, or change the structure. It is quite common to find homes with rooms, patios, and decks that have been added on. It is also more common than you might think to find that the necessary permits were not issued. You need to be aware of such potential problems before listing a property for sale. Find out if such permits were ever granted. The sellers of a 100+ year-old home in Brooklyn, New York, saw their closing delayed by nearly three months when the buyer questioned whether the back room, which was added on to the house some 75 years ago, was done with the benefit of a legal permit. A long permit search process was the result, followed by an inspection at the expense of the seller to show that the room was structurally sound.

It is advantageous to obtain all documents pertaining to the property, or at least know where they can be located. Become familiar with the means of accessing housing documents in your community. If representing buyers, make sure proper documentation for any repairs, nontypical use of the land, or change of the property's boundaries is on file. Your buyer may need to access such documents in the future should a discrepancy arise.

Real Estate Taxes

Tax on real estate, commonly known as property tax, is levied by local governments at a county or municipal level. The tax is based on the value of property, including land, and is determined by a tax assessor. The funds are used for roads, parks, schools, or other community needs as determined by the county or municipality. For your purposes, it is important to know the current real estate taxes and whether they have been raised—and by how much—in recent years. There has been a growing concern among homeowners in the few remaining states without sales tax that their property taxes have become too high and that a sales tax would ease their burden. In parts of Oregon, New Jersey, and other states, communities have challenged property tax assessments, which may be subject to administrative or judicial review. Make sure that buyers are aware of property taxes, which should be on the listing.

Down Payments and Mortgages

Sure, the wheeler dealers on late night television writing books on how to get rich in 45 minutes will tell you that you can buy a house for no money down, but in the real world most homes require a down payment. Simple put, the higher the down payment, the lower the mortgage. Most homebuyers, however, cannot put down more than 15 to 20 percent of the value of the home. The mortgage will cover the rest. Various programs are offered by the Veterans Administration, Fannie Mae, and Freddie Mac to assist homeowners who cannot afford substantial down payments. You should have an idea of where your potential buyers stand in terms of how much they can afford to spend on a home, and what they are prepared to spend as a down payment.

You should familiarize yourself with the wide variety of mortgages available and the going interest rates. Although interest rates are important, they do not represent the overall picture of a mortgage loan. There are two key areas that anyone shopping for a mortgage must consider:

1. The length of the mortgage
2. Whether the mortgage interest rate is fixed or adjustable

Fixed mortgages lock in an interest rate when the buyer purchases the loan. This is to the buyer's advantage if the interest rates are low. Adjustable rate mortgages (known as ARMs) change periodically, depending on the terms of the mortgage. The 30-year, fixed mortgage is still very popular, although there are many choices, including adjustable mortgages with balloon payments and some hybrids. Four key factors involved in the decision process are:

1. *The level of risk the buyer is willing to take.* ARMS, for instance, are more risky than fixed interest mortgages.
2. *The perceived future income of the buyers.* If their earnings are low at present but they have great earning potential (young professionals), they may take an ARM with a low interest rate now that will balloon at the end of the term of the loan.
3. *How long the buyers plan to be living in the house.* If they will be moving out in three or four years, they can benefit from an ARM with a low interest rate up front, because they will be gone before the rate goes up.
4. *The current rate of interest and how much the buyer can afford to spend monthly to pay back the mortgage.*

For buyers who plan to stay in the house for a long period of time, prefer a lower degree of risk, and are unsure of what their income-to-expense ratio will be in the future, a fixed rate loan is advisable.

Regarding the length of the loan, long-term or short-term is the question. The primary difference is that a short-term loan of 15 years will cost less money overall but will have the buyer paying more on a monthly basis, while a long-term loan of 30 years will cost more money in the long run but will keep the monthly costs lower. Because more people today are living on tighter budgets, maintaining a lower monthly rate is a common concern, and 30-year fixed rate mortgages remain in vogue. Homeowners can still reduce the costs of a long-term mortgages. They can refinance to lower rates when they are available or save money by making additional payments on the principle as they make more money or receive lump sums from bonuses or inheritances.

For your purposes, you want to know what loans are being offered and at what rates, and to be able to discuss options with buyers. Even though you are not in the business of financing, you get a better feeling for which buyers can afford which houses. You can advise buyers that they should

- have payments that fit comfortably into their budget;
- stay within a level of risk that they find acceptable;
- select a loan based, in part, by how long they plan to stay in the house.

One final note, buyers should know what they can afford, and you can help them by reminding them that the rule of thumb says they should pay no more than 28 to 33 percent of their gross monthly income toward their mortgage payment, which includes real estate taxes and homeowners' insurance.

Closing Costs

The closing is an exciting time because it means all of your hard work will actually pay off with the completed sale of the property. Costs associated with the closing are payments made by the buyer to finalize the purchase of the property. Typically, closing costs will run the buyer from 2 to 6 percent of the cost of the house.

Closing costs will vary by state and even by region or community. In some areas, it is customary that the seller pays some of the costs. Some costs can also be negotiated so the seller pays for certain costs, as agreed upon with the lender.

Some of the more common closing costs are:

- *Private mortgage insurance (PMI).* This is fairly standard. PMI is required if the down payment is less than 20 percent of the cost of the home. It protects the lender in case of a default on the loan. PMI typically costs about half of one percent of the cost of the house.
- *Title insurance.* This protects the buyer in the event someone shows up with a claim to the house.
- *Escrow deposit for taxes*
- *Loan origination fee*
- *Title company closing fee*
- *Recording fee*
- *Credit report fee*
- *Title transfer fee*

Buyers can negotiate some of the fees with their lenders. Some lenders will pick up the cost of the credit report (which is minimal), and sometimes other fees can be eliminated at the closing (although they will probably be added to the mortgage). When you first start working with the lender, you should get an estimate in writing of the closing costs. Make sure that the costs are close to the estimate, and let the lender know if they are not. The buyer will also want to have homeowners' insurance, which may be included in the closing.

Points are also due at closing. This is where, for a fee (1 percent of the cost of the house per point), the buyer can get a lower interest rate. For example, one point on a $400,000 home would be $4,000 (1 percent), which the buyer could pay at closing and it would come off of the buyer's mortgage payment. This can raise the closing costs and lower the monthly payments. It is worthwhile for a buyer who has saved a lot of money for this occasion. However, it is not always at the discretion of the buyer. Lenders will often require points based on the buyer's credit rating. A no-points loan, therefore, means a lower closing cost. Remind your buyers to shop around when considering a mortgage and to discuss closing costs with various lenders.

The Future of Your Real Estate Market

Real estate has been doing very well in recent years, at least for sellers, agents, and brokers. Buyers have had to spend more, but that does not seem to be slowing down the real estate market one bit.

Although no one can predict the future of real estate or know if the bubble is going to burst, monitor the selling prices of homes and/or businesses in your area, and keep an eye on factors that could lower real estate values, such as an escalating crime rate, overbuilding of homes or sites for businesses, or a new toxic waste dump. Improvements to the community can also raise home prices. Commercial real estate values can be dependent on increased competition, new roadways, an improved infrastructure, and/or the changing demographics of an area. The best you can do is to stay on top of the overall real estate picture by continuing to educate yourself.

Commissions

Commissions are the bread and butter of the real estate business, and like couples at dinner, your office most often shares that bread and butter with the agency representing the other party in the transaction. Therefore, you have both a buyer agency commission and a seller agency commission. Should one or both agents be part of the same franchise, such as Century 21, then the franchise also takes its cut. In other brokerage situations, agents pay a fee or a percentage of their commissions to the brokerage office for operating out of that office and utilizing its services.

If, for example, a home sells for $200,000, and the commission is 8 percent, then each office will receive 4 percent, or half of the $16,000 (8 percent of $200,000). Therefore, the seller agency receives $8,000, and the buyer agency receives

$8,000. The broker or franchise will then have a formula or a set percentage to determine how much its cut is and how much you make.

In many cases, the longer you work for a broker and the more business you bring in, the higher your percentage will be. In other cases, if both the seller and buyer agents are in the same company, you may also see a higher percentage of the commission. Commissions also vary from region to region, from office to office, and from agent to agent. They are not mandated by law and are, therefore, negotiable.

A WALK-THROUGH OF THE PROCESS OF SELLING A PROPERTY

- Meet with the seller or sellers, look over the property, do a walk-through, and make an assessment.

- If you are interested in representing the house, let the sellers know what you can do for them. They will likely talk with several agents, so this is where you need to sell yourself on why they should work with you.

- Do a comparative market analysis to determine what the listing price should be. Come up with an asking price that you believe is competitive. *Walk away from an overpriced listing if the seller won't come down to a more realistic price.*

- If the sellers agrees to work with you, they will sign a listing agreement.

- Present the agency disclosure, which lets sellers know that you have a fiduciary responsibility to them. The document should also spell out what you can and cannot legally do on their behalf.

- Do a more thorough evaluation of the property. Call in an inspector if necessary. It's due diligence time. Be thorough before listing a property.

- Get full disclosure documents signed by the seller

- Once you are comfortable that you know the property inside and out, list the property on the MLS. Fill out the form and add some outstanding things about the house in the remarks section. Prepare your listing carefully and truthfully.

- Place ads if you can afford to do so. Wording in any listing or advertisement regarding the property you are selling must be accurate, so watch what you say.

- Show the property to brokers and agents at a brokers' open house. This way they will know what they are presenting to their buyers.

- Show the property at a public open house—if you so choose—and be prepared to answer questions accordingly. (Also give out your card to visitors, and promote yourself while at an open house.)

- When you get an offer, present it to your clients in person. Discuss the offer and present your client with a sheet showing the net profits he would make after closing costs, commissions, and other fees.

- Compare several offers with your client if you get more than one.

- If you accept an offer, you will then negotiate the purchase on behalf of the seller. Review all of the buyer contingencies, most of which are standard, with your client. Be prepared to negotiate if necessary.

- If both parties sign the purchase agreement, prepare a financial settlement statement for your client.

- Represent the seller at the closing.

- Collect your commission check.

- Celebrate.

CHAPTER 6

The Work Environment
and Your
Responsibilities

PROFILE

Nancy Ferri

www.carrierrealtors.com/nancy_ferri

For more than a decade, Nancy Ferri has been winning Circle of Excellence awards from the New Jersey Association of Realtors as one of the top agents in the field. At Carrier and Associates in Brigantine, New Jersey, she has been the top seller of homes for six of the last eight years.

"I love being able to help people achieve their dreams of purchasing or selling a home," says Nancy, who moved from Westchester,

New York, to Brigantine, just off the coast of southern New Jersey, in 1979. It was Susan Carrier, owner of Carrier and Associates, who not only sold Ferri and her family a home, but also impressed Nancy. "She was professional and ethical and I knew that would be important to me," says Ferri, who decided to get her real estate license in 1988. "I was lucky to have become associated with Carrier and Associates. They gave me a desk and all the basics to get started," she recalls.

"I wanted to do something that gave me the opportunity to be there for my children and husband," explains Ferri, who appreciates the flexible hours as well as the impact of modern technology on the real estate field. "With today's technology, especially cell phones, I can stay in contact with customers and clients even when I'm not physically at the office," adds Ferri.

Based on her own success, Ferri emphasizes the need to work extremely hard in the beginning of your career, as you start generating leads and building up your contacts. "You will reap the benefits for years to come," says Ferri . In addition, she knows the importance of establishing a rapport with clients. "Even after a settlement, if a client needs some additional help, you should take the time and help them if you can. You will be so surprised how many people remember you. Referrals are the best leads you can receive," explains Nancy. She even helps clients find investment properties as well as both primary and secondary homes. "I love to help first-time home buyers," adds Ferri, who takes advantage of the great outdoors in Brigantine, playing tennis, fishing, and biking with her husband Bob in her free time. Nancy Ferri can be found at www.carrierrealtors.com/nancy_ferri.

■ ■ ■

As a newcomer to the real estate profession, you should seek out a real estate firm in which you feel comfortable. This will be your starting point in your work as an independent contractor and may launch a career that sees you move on to open your own office or even build a real estate empire. Remember that some of the nation's wealthiest people got to where they are today through significant real estate deals. Of course, you can also simply enjoy a real estate career that provides you with sufficient income while allowing you to enjoy the non-nine-to-five lifestyle.

Setting Up Your Office

If you ever stop and watch a real estate veteran in action, you'll see that she whips out the right forms from the right drawers while dealing with one customer on the phone and handing a business card to a passing customer at the same time. Organization is a key to your success. Of course, not everyone organizes in the same manner. Some people prefer a neat clean desk with everything in the appropriate drawer or nearby filing cabinet. Others maintain folders on their desks, which may look cluttered to the casual observer, but allow them to easily find whatever they need. Along with standard office supplies, you will need to have all of the necessary forms on hand, including disclosure forms and buyer and/or seller agreements. Your computer setup should be high speed, using cable or DSL access to the internet, as provided by the office. Some firms require you to foot the bill for additional technology, such as software programs or WiFi access.

While setting up your office area, also consider making it accessible for clients to comfortably sit down and discuss their needs. While a great deal of communication is done via phone calls and e-mails, try to meet clients in person and talk with them prior to working with them.

Other considerations in setting up your space include a good chair, which is very important for desk and computer work. Don't try to save money on a chair, or your back, neck, or wrists will suffer the consequences. Lighting is also important. Most offices are designed for good general lighting, but you may need to bring in your own lamp for specific workspace lighting.

Prior to declaring yourself ready for business, you need the all-important business card. Look at the cards of other real estate agents and decide what you like. Your card should stand out, and indicate clearly that you are in real estate and stand out—without being cluttered. If you can create an image visually, you should use it throughout all of your printed materials, including fliers, ads, and your letterhead stationery.

You also need to maintain numerous phone numbers. Many people use electronic organizers or software programs, and others use the old-fashioned method of writing in a phone/address book. Whatever works best for you, use it, and add to your listings regularly. Be sure to maintain a backup copy of your contact lists, because this is one of the most significant tools of the real estate trade.

One final note about your computer. Like most people in business today, you will rely heavily on your computer for accessing information and storing data on clients, properties and so on. *Back up your data often.* Have a CD or even a hard copy that you can use if the computer crashes. Technology is usually your primary assistant, but when it leaves you high and dry, you can find yourself in a major crisis. Take time to do basic computer maintenance, which means eliminating unnecessary files that are slowing your computer down. Also, get anti-virus, anti-adware, and anti-spyware software, and load it. Many offices have firewalls installed and passwords to get onto a computer system. Use their safety mechanisms, and set up some of your own. A computer virus can totally knock you out of commission, or commissions, as the case may be.

Office Expenses

Advertising, a web page on the company's site, use of the answering service, standard office supplies, and various other costs will come with the territory. Some firms pay for everything, and others charge you as much as $2,000 a month just for the privilege of being part of their offices. What a real estate office covers, regarding expenses, can vary dramatically. Many brokers agree to pay for the standard expenses of their agents, which include a web page, advertising, and basic office equipment. During the interview process you should ask which expenses will be covered and which ones will be your responsibility. Typically, dues and membership fees for organizations and associations will be an expense that you pick up. It is, however, important to become part of such organizations for lead generation purposes and training/learning opportunities.

Generating Leads

It's very simple. In real estate, you need leads to generate business. There are several ways to do this. First, you can do floor duty, also known as *opportunity time, lead time, phone duty*, and such. These are your hours to take phone calls from new customers and handle walk-ins at the firm's office. In the modern office, it may also include handling e-mails. While direct lines to agents and other advertising have cut into this means of generating leads, it is still a viable way of picking up new clients.

Be generous with your business cards and hand them out in all possible situations. Most good real estate agents have mastered the art of networking and find opportunities to meet people and hand out cards. Some people include cards in everything they send out, including their monthly bills.

Advertising is another way to generate leads but is usually too costly to do on a regular basis. However, there are ways to market yourself, which do not cost a lot of money and can be highly effective. For example, by getting your card and your name in front of the editors at local newspapers and magazines, you can become the person they call when they need a quote for a real estate article. If your community has block parties, local fairs, street fairs, or other such gatherings, it is usually very easy and inexpensive to sponsor an activity or have a handout such as balloons with your company name on them. There are numerous ways to get yourself, or your name, in front of people. Attend trade shows and community meetings, and make yourself known within the area you represent.

There are also lead generating services, particularly on the internet. However, you need to be careful. Legitimate lead-generating services gather leads themselves for various clients, such as yourself, in a reputable manner by advertising on search engines or having people sign up with their services. Conversely, other services use everything from spam and pop-up ads to a variety of other tricks to generate what are considered garbage leads because the person signing up does not know what he signed up for. Make sure you get a good referral from someone who has had success working through a lead generating service before you sign up with one.

Web sites are always a good way for generating leads. You can certainly set up your own web page, or if you are working for a large firm, it may provide you with a web page. However, a good-looking, well-designed web page is meaningless unless you market it so that people will find you. Here, you can do several things. First, you can trade links with other local businesses that have a web presence or barter— you advertise for them and they advertise for you. You should also make sure that any advertising you have, from business cards to fliers to pens, has your e-mail address on it.

Next, you can use viral marketing to try to generate more leads. Viral marketing is where you use the power of word-of-mouth in your favor. The trick is to provide those who come to your web site with something that makes them forward your e-mail to a friend. For example, people enjoy sharing jokes, recipes, or sending e-cards for special occasions. Anything that you can provide that can launch a viral marketing campaign will generate free advertising. You can also offer a finder's reward of some sort, so that anyone who forwards your name to a friend, who ends up buying/selling a property from you, can receive a gift. The keys to good online viral marketing are

- giving people something they want to share with other people.

- making sure it is easy to forward the information to a friend on one click.
- having such material in a hot spot (highly visible location) on your web site.

All of these are ways to bring attention to yourself as a salesperson. However, if you really want to move ahead of the pack, you will hone a more strategic lead generation system.

Because sellers provide your commissions in most markets and are less of a hit-or-miss proposition than showing buyers numerous houses, you may emphasize the selling aspect of your business. To generate seller leads, you need to find a proactive manner of locating and marketing yourself to people looking to sell their homes. One way of doing so is directing your attention to the demographic groups that are most likely to sell their houses and then targeting them as your prime audience.

Research shows that a good percentage of the people who start out selling homes themselves will ultimately end up with a real estate agent working with them. Why shouldn't that person be you? Try marketing yourself to people selling their homes that have signs on their lawns, ads in the newspapers, or postings on web sites that say: "For Sale by Owner." The MLS provides expired listings everyday, and you can also go to web sites such as www.forsalebyowner.com, among others (see the web sites in the Appendix). You can scan the local papers and even ask the people you do business with in the community to let you know if they see such a sign on a property.

When marketing to such groups, you need to first consider if they made conscious decisions to sell their homes without an agent or broker. If so, contacting them is proceeding contrary to the sales route that they chose. To present yourself in a more positive manner, you need to offer them something or several things that you can do for them that they cannot do for themselves. For example, perhaps you can provide a free consultation with an investment advisor—arrange this in advance with an advisor who can benefit from your sale by having a potential new client with money to invest. Can you align yourself with a mover that can give a discount? Again, you are getting business for them in a barter situation. Of course, you can also offer the things that you as an agent can do, such as a free analysis of potential buyers or running an open house for them (which includes sending out invitations and even having refreshments available). By presenting the home seller with reasons why your services may be of benefit to them, you position yourself as the logical alternative should he not be able to sell his home on his own.

Use direct mail to reach your target audience and follow up shortly thereafter. Be aggressive but not intrusive. While it's true that many of these sellers, perhaps 90 percent, will not want to do business with you, 10 percent of these leads may yield results. Typically, cold calling or random marketing efforts yield less than a 3 percent response rate. Therefore, you are already positioning yourself to outpace your competition. There are numerous other ways to define specific demographic groups for lead generation. Some possibilities are discussed in Chapter 7. Being proactive in the real estate business and going after targeted leads separates the $40,000 earners from the $100,000 earners.

Floor Duty

As mentioned earlier, floor duty—which goes by various names—entails being one of the agents responsible for handling the phones and walk-in customers. This time presents a valuable opportunity to gather leads. Your personality and professionalism are key factors in being successful here. It is up to you to find out what callers are seeking and to begin a relationship, starting with an initial meeting. Make it clear that there is no obligation to work with you, but that you are very familiar with the neighborhood and would be happy to discuss their needs. Present what separates you from other real estate agents without being overly aggressive.

In areas where there is not a great deal of walk-in business, some sales agents handle phone time off premises. Most firms have an ongoing rotating schedule whereby all of the agents affiliated with the office handle a certain amount of phone duty each week.

Are You a Team Player?

Like it or not, real estate is a competitive business. Although you are all under one roof, you are independent contractors. You may find competition in your office. This, however, is not always the case. Some offices develop a degree of camaraderie and a sense of teamwork based on the fact that you are all essentially selling homes in the same general vicinity, and if you are fair about dividing up leads, there should be no reason to compete with one another . . . *or at least not on the surface.*

In offices where a team atmosphere has been encouraged, agents share their knowledge, and seasoned pros are willing to help the newer agents get off and running. After all, there are only so many clients one agent can take on at a given time, and sub-agent commissions may emerge from helping each another handle an overflow. When looking for a real estate firm in which to work, you will want to see what the relationships are among the agents and between the agents and the office manager. A team atmosphere can build your enthusiasm for the business. As a new agent, you can not only learn from the senior members of the firm but also offer to assist them and be helpful while building a collegial relationship. In some cases, you may cover for another agent who cannot be in two places at once and show properties to buyers for her. Such teamwork usually will result in a decision to split the commission if a sale is made. Brokers like to encourage such teamwork to keep customers satisfied and referrals coming into the business.

Handling the Competition

Brokers who run real estate firms typically have to deal more with competition from other firms than among agents.

Running a real estate firm, like running any type of business, means seeking ways to give yourself a competitive edge by providing something the competition does not offer. At the agent level, it's also useful to find a competitive edge.

In an age of impersonal high-tech communications, going the extra mile to be the more client-friendly business by providing personal attention sometimes pays off generously—especially in a people-oriented field like residential real estate. One homebuyer, when asked why he chose between two agents with whom he and his family toured several houses, responded, "We had our kids with us, and one agent was very friendly to them and understood that moving and house hunting was a difficult time for kids. The other acted like they weren't even there. So, we went with the first agent, and she helped us find the house we are living in today."

It's a people-oriented business, and the companies that are able to focus more closely on the needs of their audience as individuals are going to succeed. Even in commercial real estate, customer service and good interaction with people is still highly valued.

To handle the competition successfully, you need to stay on top of what other agents and other firms are doing. Visit other open houses, read literature about competitive firms, and visit other web sites. Know what the competition is doing—and especially what they are not doing—because that is where you can find your strength or niche.

Fiduciary Responsibility

Typically, we associate fiduciary responsibility with the investment field. However, the purchase of a home, a business establishment, or raw land is a major investment, and the modern day real estate agent needs to be held accountable. Therefore, real estate agents and brokers must always be careful to act in the best interests of their clients, particularly in a society that feeds on the potential for lawsuits.

A real estate agent can be held liable for any number of discrepancies, especially if there is a problem with the property that the selling agent knew about but did not disclose or misrepresented. For this reason, numerous disclosures and contracts are part of the process of purchasing real estate.

There are also situations in which an agent may represent both a seller and a buyer of a property. In some states this is not permitted, and some firms have policies that call for a second agent to be involved. If an agent is acting as a dual agent, that dual status must be in writing and agreed upon by both the buyer and the seller. In addition, the agent must provide each side with accurate information. (There is still some debate surrounding the merits of dual agency.)

Acting with integrity, honesty, and in a professional manner at all times should help you honor your fiduciary responsibility to your clients.

Errors and Omissions (E&O) Insurance

Fiduciary responsibility goes hand in hand with the potential for liability. Even if you are careful to disclose all of the information that you know about a property, as an agent or a broker with agents working for you, it is possible to be held accountable should information be found to be incorrect or omitted during the sale of the property. Once contracts are signed, a client may feel that you failed to adhere to your responsibilities according to that contract. E&O insurance can protect you in the event a client files a lawsuit for those reasons. It will pay up to the limit of your coverage, including court costs should these occur. Generally, you pay to be covered under the broker's policy. Liability insurance typically does not cover such errors, making it very important to have E&O insurance.

Discrimination and Fair Housing Laws

One of the primary objectives of the U.S. Department of Housing and Urban Development was to establish and enforce fair housing laws. Today, such laws not only exist but are carefully watched. Both agents and brokers can have their licenses suspended if they are found to be discriminating in their business practices. Not only is discrimination not tolerated in regard to individuals, but you cannot draw conclusions for buyers (or sellers), such as telling them that the schools in a certain neighborhood are not very good. You can

only recommend that buyers read informative web sites or literature and draw their own conclusions. In addition, you cannot steer clients away from, or toward, certain neighborhoods based on race, religion, or ethnicity.

Multiple Listing Service

The most important technical necessity for a real estate agent in the 21st century is still the Multiple Listing Service (MLS). Every area has such a service that provides comprehensive listings of all properties that come onto the market for sale or for rent. You will also use the MLS for your clients who are looking to sell or rent their properties. The service typically provides details of the properties listed, a photo, the asking price, and contact information for the listing agent. Property taxes, school district, and other local information is also usually provided. You must take some time to familiarize yourself with the MLS and learn how to list as well as what other data is available. You can usually find a wide range of neighborhood statistics.

Along with posting listings, the MLS should be your guide to searching for properties. Once you are familiar with using the MLS to search by specific criteria, you will be able to quickly locate properties that meet the needs of prospective buyers.

Disclosures and Waivers

A seller's disclosure is a detailed account of the history of the property, including any problems with the roofing, plumbing, septic system, and so on. This information is to protect the buyer from the old-fashioned "buyer beware" policy that no longer exists in real estate.

Buyers, meanwhile, should be advised to conduct any and all inspections that they deem necessary for a particular property. Inspection contingencies are common prior to closing on a property. Today, inspections include those looking for structural abnormalities and the general condition of the property as well as those for termites, radon, lead paint, and other health or environmental concerns. Sellers typically pay for inspections. Buyers can decide not to have a specific inspection conducted and sign a waiver, which is kept on file, stating that they chose not to have the inspection done.

Make sure you have disclosure and waiver forms available at all times so that you have in writing what is known about a property and what has been offered, waived, or bypassed.

Virtual Tours

Once upon a time, you literally had to visit each and every property. Today, through the wonders of technology, virtual tours can expedite the search process (to some degree) by showing buyers both the interior and exterior of a property. The process of taking photos and setting up a virtual tour has become very simple and the practice of using such virtual tours as an option is broadening. While properties won't sell on the basis of a virtual tour, such a high-tech visit can weed out those properties that are simply "not right." Prospective homebuyers can look at a number of houses using the virtual tour and narrow down the list to the few that they want to visit. There are companies that specifically create such virtual tours; however, they can be costly. There are also firms that essentially create their own tours by uploading digital photographs taken of the properties.

The Industry Open House

When a house is about to be listed, the seller's agent typically sets aside a day on which real estate agents and brokers can tour the property to familiarize themselves with what they hope to be showing prospective buyers. As the seller's agent, you need to be very familiar with house, having reviewed everything from the seller (and the disclosure form he has filled out). You then need to schedule the open house, prepare to answer questions from your fellow agents, and provide as much data as you have on the property.

When touring homes as a potential buyers' agent, it is your opportunity to familiarize yourself with all of the details (take notes) so that when you show prospective buyers around, you will sound confident in your knowledge of the property.

The Public Open House

One way of letting as many potential buyers as possible see a property is by arranging for an open house for the public. If you plan to hold an open house, you will typically list the date of the open house when you enter your listing with the MLS. This alerts other agents to the open house so they can let prospective buyers know.

However, this open house is for the public and you need to focus more attention on drawing such potential buyers directly. Advertising is important, and typically local signage is the best means of spreading the word. Posting notices on local bulletin boards in stores and laundry facilities also draws attention. Make sure you schedule an open house on a weekend and avoid holidays when your turnout may be limited because people are out of town. Also, keep the sellers busy that day so they won't be in the middle of the activity.

Typically, sales are not made at open houses. However, with open houses you can accomplish several things. First, you can pique the interest of potential buyers. Second, you can promote yourself as a real estate agent in the area, and third, you can promote the firm at which you work.

Set defined start and end times for the open house and have everyone off of the property before sundown. If there are too many visitors, let some people know that they have to wait before entering. You need to be able to clearly see who is in the house and pay close attention to their activities. You also want to answer questions in a concise manner so that you do not become preoccupied with one person, or couple, at the expense of ignoring others who may be interested in the property.

The reality, of course, is that many of the people coming to an open house are not there to buy a home. Sellers, interested neighbors, and others who may want to see what homes in the area look like may all be among your guests. You never know, however, who is a potential buyer or who has a friend who needs the services of a real estate agent.

Research

The modern real estate agent is frequently found using the internet for research. Many county courthouses provide web sites for researching documents, while other local area web sites can be helpful for verifying facts. You can use the internet searches in conjunction with other means of research to find targeted leads. Generating leads from the web can also help you locate a market of potential buyers or sellers in your area. For example, you can locate a rental area with numerous young professional couples who may be ready to go from renting an apartment to buying a home.

Despite all of the latest technology, there is also the occasional need to rummage through files for old documents. However, it is important to remember that while doing research, you need to check dates to make sure the information is accurate, and in the case of the web, updated, current, and correct.

SAFETY ISSUES

One of the unfortunate realities of the real estate business is that there are some legitimate safety concerns. Using common sense safety measures are typically your best defense.

In their enthusiasm to show prospective buyers around houses, real estate agents have found themselves alone with strangers who ended up robbing, raping, or even murdering them. The numbers are very minimal, so you need not panic. Nonetheless, you should take some precautions. First, have your cell phone on you whenever showing a property, and have one button programmed for the nearby police precinct. You should show homes during daytime hours and always use your car. Make sure someone in your office knows where you are going.

It is also a good idea to always try to maintain a clear path to an exit. While showing rooms on the main floor, stand at the doorway of rooms located upstairs, and do not accompany your prospective buyer to the basement or attic.

When showing more than one person around, be aware of where each person is in the house. It is not uncommon for a couple to split up when looking at the home. One person engages the agent in conversation and asks plenty of questions, while the other person takes jewelry or other valuable items. This crime is more common than crimes against agents.

You also need to be aware of your surroundings at all times. When you arrive at a destination, take a moment to look around. If you see anything suspicious, you may not want to visit the property right then. Make sure you park in an area where you will not get blocked in by other cars. When showing a house, make sure when you first arrive that no unfamiliar person is on the property. The listing agent should let you know who the owners are and whom to expect when you visit. Also, don't show open houses alone; instead have another agent or someone from the office accompany you.

Numerous real estate professionals have been in the business for many years without any problems. However, to play it safe, be aware, and take such precautions.

■   ■   ■

Try Before
You Buy

David Fischer

Talking with a Former Intern Who Is
Now in the Real Estate Field

David Fischer first interned between his soph-
omore and junior years at the University of
Georgia, where he studied commercial real estate at the Terry
School of Business. The first of two internships was in a small company where he handled various assignments for several people in
the office. "I got an overview of all that is out there in the real estate
business," says David, who sat in at client meetings and got an

inside look at how the commercial real estate business works. "Classes made so much more sense after that. I felt that it put me one step ahead of the game," he explains.

After his junior year, he wanted to work for another company to see the business from another vantage point. This time he worked for the finance division of a much larger company and learned how real estate deals are financed. "As I look at it, once you know financing you will understand so much more about the business," explains Fischer, who was hired right after school by Bank of America, where he immediately went into one of its training programs.

Fischer highly recommends internships as an ideal means of getting a foot in the door, learning about the profession, and meeting people. "The person who hired me, it turns out, was friends with the president of the company that I had interned with the previous summer," he says. "It's very much a matter of meeting people and getting to know them in this business," he adds, noting that the field becomes very small in a given market, even one the size of Atlanta, where the top players all know each other. While in the training program, he is now meeting many of these major players in the Atlanta real estate market.

In addition to his Bank of America position, Fischer, at just 23, is a partner in a small real estate business with his brother. They own a couple of properties at present and hope to build the business steadily by purchasing additional residential properties each year and eventually developing these and other properties.

■ ■ ■

You've probably heard the suggestion that before you purchase a home in an area far from where you currently reside, you should try renting for a while to see if you like the community. Renting for a year can allow you to familiarize yourself with the lay of the land. The same holds true for finding a job. After all, just like people plan to stay in a home, most people also plan to be at their chosen careers for a while. Internships, temporary employment, and part-time positions can all provide initial training and an opportunity to familiarize yourself with what it is like on the inside of a real estate firm. Such on-the-job training can prove very valuable.

Internships and Part-Time Jobs

Internships have evolved as a rich and rewarding educational experience for high school and college students wishing to learn about a career in a professional environment. There are numerous stories of students developing their skills through internships and landing full-time jobs in the company where they interned. Real estate interns assist in research, managing properties, closings, showings, listing properties, accounting and office functions, and numerous other areas.

Those who have had internships say that they learned a lot from watching real business situations unfold in the office environment. The manner in which situations are handled and problems are dealt with can provide invaluable learning experience. In addition, internships can, and often do, lead to valuable contacts in the industry. Even situations that do not lead directly to employment can result in very positive letters of reference or referrals to other businesses looking for new talent. Because interns are not in competition with agents or brokers, they should ask plenty of questions to gain a better understanding of the process.

Many colleges offer real estate internships. Typically, the school affiliates with area businesses and offers a certain number of credits per term, providing the intern works at least the minimum number of hours required. Tuition is typically paid for the number of credits, in the same manner as taking a three- or four-credit course. Some interns also receive pay for their work, but generally the salaries are low. All of the specifics depend upon the college, its program, and the participating companies.

Internships can usually be found to meet the specific interests of the students, such as real estate law or property management. Students who enter real estate internships should have good interpersonal and communication skills, and meet the requirements of the hiring company. Some actual listings from companies seeking interns follow. They provide a glimpse of what the companies are looking for when seeking interns.

- *CB Real Estate Corporation.* Student learns entire process of real estate transactions in an established internship program where student interns are assigned to a specific agent; comprehensive program.
- *CSC Real Estate.* Escrow division seeks intern with good communication skills verbally and writing, good computer skills, and ability to multitask; $9.50 per hour.
- *ITG Appraisers.* Student learns appraisal software and all aspects to become a qualified appraiser; $5 per hour.
- *ERA Properties.* Student will learn all aspects of real estate as assistant to owner; word processing and internet skills necessary; incentive program to be arranged.

In general the majority of students find internships valuable because they provide real life training. Some go into the profession; others learn that they do not want to work in the specific industry.

Part-time employment is another way to "try" a chosen field. However, such positions are often harder to find and typically do not come with the same level of enthusiasm from co-workers who often have a more cynical view of part-timers than of interns. Often, part-timers are seen as not taking their careers as seriously, although this is not usually the case.

The positives about part-time work in real estate are that you can get your feet wet while learning the business, making some money, and still going to school in preparation for your licensing exam. Below is a sample part-time job listing from the real estate section of a major internet employment web site:

Stimulating opportunity for outgoing and determined individual. Approximately 20 hours a week. We are seeking someone who is accustomed to meeting deadlines, handling a lot of paperwork, and is comfortable working with the general public. Must have great people skills and be well-versed in Publisher, Word, Internet Base Programs, and Excel. You will also need to be familiar with using a digital camera, scanner, color printer, and other basic office equipment. Please send resume to . . .

Such a position may include posting listings, taking digital photographs for virtual home tours, and greeting people at an open house. As a part-timer, you can work flexible hours and get a taste of what working in the field entails.

Finding part-time work can be more difficult than finding full-time work. For that reason, it is to your advantage to take the initiative and write letters to local real estate firms explaining that you are seeking part-time employment and providing a resume or at least a list of your skills. Don't sit back and look for part-time job listings. Instead, do some networking. Talk to people in real estate. Find out who knows a real estate agent, and try to get your name in front of people in the industry. Let them know how they can benefit from your skills on a part-time basis. Also, let them know if you are pursuing a real estate career on a full-time basis after completing your course work.

Mentors and Learning from Professionals

Mentors are defined as wise or trusted counselors, or teachers, from whom you can learn. The concept is to have a one-to-one personal educational experience in which the more experienced, knowledgeable professional trains the younger, newer student of a particular business or craft. This can range from the real estate industry to becoming a Jedi Knight. Some mentors evolve from personal relationships while others are hired as personal teachers.

The problem is that before you can learn from a mentor, coach, or "guru," you need to find one who will teach you and not take advantage of you. In today's competitive society, there is a growing breed of opportunists. Therefore, a real estate mentor should be working *with* you and not just filtering information to you, particularly information that you can easily find elsewhere. For this reason, actually hiring a mentor or coach is advisable after you have learned the basics of the industry and even after you have gained a year or two of experience. Walter Sanford was one of the nation's leading sellers of real estate through the 1980s and 1990s and today heads Sanford Systems and Strategies and speaks worldwide on real estate. He says you don't need to hire a coach prematurely.

"My recommendation personally is that before you hire a coach, you should get the basics down. Get a basic lead-generation system for sellers, get a basic system on how you work with buyers, get basic marketing and closing checklists down, get a couple of years of experience under your belt," says Sanford. "Mentors don't want to teach people the basics . . . that can be found in books (including several by Sanford, one of which is *Expert Lead Generation Tool Kit*). Read that stuff and follow it." He says most major real estate firms, such as Century 21 or the Coldwell Banker, provide enough training to get you to that $100,000 earnings mark. "It's going beyond that training where getting a mentor or a coach may be valuable," adds Sanford.

In the early stages, Sanford recommends tapping into the knowledge of the top sellers in your area:

> *Your goal is to find the things in real estate that work at the least cost and in the shortest amount of time. Real estate is a fairly mature industry, which means most of the stuff that works has been discovered and all we're doing now is applying technology to old ideas to make them less expensive and faster in their implementation and in their end results.*

He believes that by seeking out the people who are at the top of their game for a short interview (over lunch or for a cup of coffee), you can learn a lot. "People like this are proud of their accomplishments and happy to share some of their ideas, but you should be armed with a few key questions." (See Figure 7.1.)

FIGURE 7.1

Questions to Ask Professionals

What do you ask when you find someone who is willing to coach, mentor, or simply provide some advice? Here are ten questions you might consider asking top professionals in the field.

1. What do you feel is the most cost-effective, proactive means of generating seller leads?

2. How do you go ahead and handle the problem of commission negotiation?

3. How frequently do you follow up on leads?

4. How do you know when to stop yourself from taking an over-priced listing?

5. How can you tell a good potential buyer from an unlikely buyer?

6. Are there good methods you recommend to increase buyer leads?

7. Which methods of marketing do you recommend?

8. How do you read your customer so that you can adapt your communications appropriately?

9. What is the best way to maintain customer relationships over the years?

10. Are there any specific sources, such as periodicals or web sites, that you recommend for a new real estate agent?

As a new agent, your goal is to copy successful lead-generation systems, checklists, listing strategies, buyer satisfaction tools, and all of the other tools that have been learned over the years and honed by the pros, like Sanford, through the hard knocks and realities of being in the business.

If you do pay for advice, whether it is a coach, a mentor, or a seminar, be careful from whom you are taking advice. Remember, in a field such as real estate, there is no one-size-fits-all approach, which should eliminate most of the gurus with the get-rich-quick gimmicks. These are individuals who teach their own methods, some of which may border on illegality. Be wary of anyone who claims to have "the fool-proof formula" for making a fortune in real estate.

A good mentor or coach should be defined by what you walk away with, not by his credentials or previous credits. Yes, you want to know in advance that someone has a background in the industry and has sold real estate, particularly in your area. However, too many people confuse letters after someone's name with actual knowledge and hands-on experience. A real estate agent with 20 years in the field will very likely teach you as much, if not a lot more, than someone with a Ph.D. and various other credentials who has little or no real world experience. It is important that you find someone who recognizes your strengths and abilities and works with what you have. It is also important that the individual knows what you will be able to accomplish in your chosen territory.

Unrealistic goals, whether set by you or someone else, are a waste of time.

Typically, the best way to learn from professionals is to go out and find them, meet them, and become part of their world. Attend conventions and conference seminars. Find out where the local real estate professionals hang out. You should also attend open houses and go wherever you think you may be able to mingle with successful professionals from whom you can learn. Some of these people will shun you, others will be cordial. Those who are comfortable with themselves will often be the most helpful and forthcoming about their business strategies, knowing that as the wide-eyed newcomer, you do not pose a competitive threat.

To benefit from professional wisdom, you need to be observant, pay attention, ask questions, and listen carefully to the answers you receive. If you are fortunate enough to talk with a variety of veteran real estate professionals, you can compare their responses as well as their systems and strategies. By taking good notes and making comparisons, you can develop your own systems and strategies based on what you've learned and what will work best in your geographic area or with a specific demographic group.

Conventions and Newsletters

Conventions provide a nice atmosphere for meeting sales agents from other areas who can openly share ideas with you, knowing you are not in direct competition for the same business. In

addition, you can learn a lot from speakers at conventions, conferences, and seminars.

Keep in mind that learning is not only reserved for new-comers in the field. No matter how long you work as an agent, broker, or in any aspect of real estate, you will need to keep up with changes and new developments in the industry.

Newsletters are also great sources for learning about such conferences and seminars, and typically have short articles and tips that you can learn from. E-mail newsletters are plentiful in most industries, including real estate.

Professional Wisdom

Real estate is a business, and like all businesses, professionals will recommend that you seek out cost-effective means of reaching your goal—making sales. If you can construct a system that saves you time and cuts to the chase—such as weeding out interested buyers and sellers from those who are just speculating, or a system of generating targeted leads—you'll be better off. The 30-year pros like Walter Sanford will tell you to focus on finding sellers so that you have an inventory and find a demographic audience that has the best results. For example, rather than cold calling or trying to use the data from an entire neighborhood to determine who is most likely to sell their homes, gather data on a specific demographic group. Check out groups such as people over 30 who are getting married and may be selling one of their homes, empty nesters looking to move to smaller homes, or recent retirees who may be moving to Florida or Arizona. These are examples of demographic groups that are more likely to sell homes. If, for example, you selected these as three demographic target groups, you could then do your research and find a way to market to these people effectively rather than doing direct mass marketing. Note: Learn which demographic groups are prevalent in your region.

Another bit of professional wisdom in business (in general) is always offering your potential customers something of value. You want to grab the attention of your demographic groups. E-mail newsletters, for example, are frequently used by businesses to provide quality content—something of value to potential customers. The basic idea is the same as that of buying a newspaper or magazine. You are essentially making a deal whereby you provide content but also advertise your services. Readers accept your advertising because they are getting quality something in return. People don't mind reading a magazine, newspaper, or your e-mail because they are also receiving articles, reviews, listings of information, puzzles, games, content that is of benefit to them. They wouldn't pay for a newspaper or magazine if it did not have any content or valuable information. In the same manner, people will not sign on for your e-mail newsletter if they are only going to receive ads. (Of course you need permission from each person before you send a newsletter or any e-mail. You never want to spam anyone.) Therefore, provide a very brief article or two of interest to your demographic group each week, plus your marketing material. Then, when they are ready to move, they will remember your name. This is just one of many ways to provide information of value to customers and establish a relationship with them.

Walter Sanford says that he sends direct mailings and follows up with phone calls to his demographic groups. He provides as many as 15 potential direct benefits that he can offer them. You need to know what is of value to your potential customers and then offer it to them.

It is this kind of business and sales wisdom that you can gain from talking with professionals who have been in the field for years. They have worked their systems, generated quality leads, and made sales. There are systems in place for all areas of real estate, and you can tap into them by seeking out professionals and learning from them.

Once you get a system in place, streamline it so that you use technology effectively and eventually take on assistants, part-timers, or interns to work the system while you move on to finding another target demographic market. One of your most important goals should be freeing yourself up from doing basic office work so that you can grow your business by building new systems and finding new means of lead generation.

CHAPTER 8

Getting
Hired

PROFILE
Janet Brand
Starting Out

Janet Brand, now an associate broker for Houlihan Lawrence, has been in real estate for 25 years. "I guess selling was in my blood," she says with a laugh. Janet was working as a schoolteacher when she started in real estate. She heeded the warning that you should not quit your day job to go into real estate unless you have at least six months of savings to tide you over.

After buying her first home, with her husband, and before having kids, she would go from the school to the real estate office and put in time on weekends. "After a while, I was earning more money in real estate than from teaching," says Janet, who then left teaching to devote all of her time to real estate.

Some two decades later, she still enjoys what she does. "It doesn't get boring because no two transactions are ever alike," says Janet. "I also like the idea of helping people find their dream homes." Janet believes that you need to approach real estate with the idea of performing a service and doing a thorough job. "You can't go into this field thinking, 'I'm going to make a lot of money.' You may end up making lots of money, but you first have to think about providing a service for people and establishing relationships."

■   ■   ■

So, you're ready to step into the world of real estate. Are you confident of your skills? Your knowledge? Your abilities? The first step before seeking a job in any field is self-evaluation, followed by actual job-hunting process.

Evaluating Your Appropriate Experience and Skills

When entering a new field, you will clearly have limited experience. Therefore, you need to look at other experiences which you can draw upon. For example, if you have phone and communications skills from past jobs or even volunteer or internship positions, they can be of benefit. Your computer experience, particularly in online research, is advantageous.

What you need to do is make a list of skills that you believe are necessary in the real estate industry, and for each one, rate your skill level from one to ten, ten being the areas in which you feel that you excel the most. Be brutally honest. If you feel your knowledge and abilities in a particular area are weak, then rate them lower. When you are finished, check off your highest skills, and focus on how you can improve the skills you rated poorly. These are the skills you will need to hone before jumping into the field. You will certainly learn specifics on the job, but you need to have a comfortable skill level when you enter the field so that you can focus on growing your business rather than improving your skills while you are working.

Hone Your Pre-Interview Skills

While you will receive training in the methods used by a specific firm, you want to hit the ground running. To do so, you may want to take some time developing your skills before your interviews. Some topics to include as you consider the areas that need improvement include:

- *Negotiating.* Books and seminars are widely available in this area.

- *People skills.* These are best polished by interacting with people on a regular basis. Volunteer in a school, church, temple, hospital, or at locations where you can interact with a variety of people on a regular basis.
- *Sales skills.* Because selling involves interaction with other people, to improve your sales skills you need to find opportunities to interact in your neighborhood, perhaps through a neighborhood fundraising campaign at a school or charitable organization. In addition, you can learn about sales from seminars and books.
- *Technical skills.* There are plenty of books and CDs available to help you familiarize yourself with software programs. Practice your research skills on the computer by trying to track down demographic statistical information in your area.

Study Real Estate Listings

If you are selling real estate, you need to know how to list properties. One of the simplest ways of doing this is by finding as many listings as possible and comparing them: What do they say and why? How are they worded? What is omitted? Whether you are representing sellers or buyers, you need to understand the meaning of each mention on a listing and be able to explain why it is there. Listings are a constant part of your life as a real estate professional, so reading them should become second nature to you.

Finding Your Niche

If you put your name out there and sit back waiting for business to come to you, it may be a long wait. If, however, you are proactive, then you can find your niche. By carving your own niche, you can gain a higher percentage of the market than by being just one of the pack. Therefore, you need to zero in on specific demographic groups and "own them."

To find your niche, you need to know the neighborhood(s), know the market, and know with whom you communicate well. In some instances, you can capitalize on who you are and which demographic group you fall into. For example, a young married real estate professional, with kids, living in a major city such as New York, might look at the growing number of families with young children. These families are quickly outgrowing those condos and want to sell and relocate to larger homes in the suburbs, something you can relate to personally. If you are an empty nester who has sold a larger home to buy something smaller and easier to take care of, then you will relate with other empty nesters and meet them in your own circle within the community. The number of home sellers in this group (typically people in their 50s and early 60s) is more than 5 percent higher than any other demographic group when it comes to selling homes. As one real estate agent explained about demographics, "Being a mom with kids, buyers who are looking for a home that's great for kids are comfortable with what I can offer them, since I'm in a similar place myself."

You might have a business background and know about the companies that are moving to and from areas. You can then work your way into the relocation market, which is a very profitable niche. Use your own knowledge and sphere of influence.

When interviewing, in addition to finding out as much as you can about the firm, let the broker or recruiter know that you have plans to build your business. An agent with a game plan to generate leads, create a niche, and utilize his or her sphere of influence is much more likely to be recruited than someone who has no plans.

Finding Real Estate Job Openings

There is no special secret to finding out about real estate job openings. Because you need a sponsor before taking your licensing exam, you actually start establishing your contacts before you attend classes, and in many cases have a place to start working once you are licensed.

Of course, you may not necessarily work for the firm that sponsored you, or you may want to switch firms after getting your feet wet. Many real estate agents turn to the person who sold them their own home for their initial contacts. Others turn to friends and relatives who have purchased homes. It's easy to come in contact with at least one real estate agent, if not several, through word of mouth and by being mildly aggressive. You could even tour some open houses and ask the agents showing the houses if you could contact them at a later date

If, however, you want to get a foot in the door even before taking your licensing exam and learn about the business while working in some capacity in a real estate office, you can employ the usual proactive job-seeking methods. First, go to the sources, such as the firms in your neighborhood and see what is available. Go online and look at local job listings as well as the websites of the real estate businesses in your area. Being proactive means talking to people who are directly in the business, such as agents or brokers, as well as other people who are indirectly involved in real estate, such as contractors or inspectors. The chamber of commerce, along with other local business organizations or associations, may have listings of new businesses. Look for new real estate businesses that have either recently opened or moved into your area. Spread the word that you are looking for a job in real estate to anyone who may come in contact with people in the industry. Then, of course, there are always the job ads in the local papers. However, it's far more advantageous for you to network.

Acing the Interview

There are more than two million people in the United States working as real estate agents or brokers, and the number has increased by more than 15 percent over the last ten years. While the numbers are likely to level off, there is still great interest in real estate as a career.

Real estate job hunting is a different animal for three primary reasons.

1. You are essentially an independent contractor, meaning the employer is not investing the same money in hiring you as would be the case in a more traditional hiring situation. In fact, you may be paying to rent space and chipping in for advertising and other services. Therefore, as discussed earlier, interviewing is often a two-way street. You are also deciding whether or not a firm is to your liking.

2. There is a steady turnover rate. Many new agents jump into the field seeing big sales and big dollars, not realizing that the first six months to one year is very often a losing financial situation. Therefore, they leave rather than sticking it out.

3. You should have a firm already in your corner because you were sponsored to take the licensing exam.

Being new to the field, you need to think through each aspect of real estate carefully in advance and even take some notes. It's not a matter of trying to guess what the interviewer wants to hear, but a matter of presenting the right qualities for the real estate industry (discussed in Chapter 2), as well as having a plan for your business.

For a broker to bring you into her or his firm, you should exhibit the discipline necessary to increase the sales revenues of that office. You need to demonstrate that you have both the determination and the knowledge of how the industry operates.

It's a combination of being ready to answer questions and asking those that are important. For example, an agent should inquire about training, expenses (what is covered by the firm and what you will cover), and how advertising is handled. Be prepared to offer your own ideas.

Think through the manner in which you will run your business. In Chapter 10, you will find a business plan for brokers opening an office. You need not create an entire business plan, but it is worthwhile to make up an abbreviated version including your goals, a summary of how your operation will work, and the progression you see from starting out until you anticipate turning a profit. The better prepared you are in regard to running your business within the business, the more impressed a broker will be with your responses. Remember, be realistic and don't exaggerate in your micro-business plan.

Interview Tips

In preparing for an interview, question yourself.

- Are you a people person? Explain why.
- Can you sell? Explain why you believe you can.
- Do you have attention to detail? Again, explain why.
- Have you done research?
- Are you comfortable with a flexible schedule?
- Why did you want to go into real estate?
- How do you define real estate? (Remember, it's much more than just selling homes.)

- What skills do you have that will be applicable in the field?

It's important to be realistic and not focus on money as your primary objective. If you do well, the money will be there. When you start out, you need to show that you are anxious to learn the business and provide a service.

The following ten tips will help you stay focused and have a successful interview:

1. *Don't be negative.* You're not going into real estate because you hate your current job, nor do you have anything negative to say about other real estate firms.

2. *Don't think of real estate as a "sideline."* It's a real full-time business, not something to do when you have free time.

3. *Don't be overconfident.* "I can sell anything" is a blatant lie. Nobody can sell anything.

4. *Don't talk too much.* Rambling shows nervousness. Often the person who talks endlessly sounds like he is trying to make himself believe what he is saying.

5. *Listen.* If you don't hear the question, you can't answer it properly. Also, the interviewer may explain what she is looking for. Determine whether or not that is you.

6. *Avoid going off on tangents.* Listen to yourself. If you hear yourself talking about your daughter's homework assignment, tell yourself to shut up.

7. *Don't try to act like you know real estate inside out.* Remember, you're new to the field.

8. *Don't exaggerate technical skills.* Even if you are very good on certain computer programs, don't act like the "expert." It's probable that you will be nervous in a new environment and not appear as the high-tech genius you make yourself out to be.

9. *Use skills from previous jobs or schooling as examples of what you can bring to real estate.*

10. *Remember your manners.* Dress properly, make eye contact, don't slouch, shake hands when you enter and leave the room, and do all of the basics you've probably heard before regarding politeness and poise during an interview.

Getting
Ahead

After losing her husband, Jean Warkala, of Brigantine, New Jersey, knew that she had to return to work. Jean started off as a secretary working at real estate offices, but soon knew she wanted to do more. So she took the necessary courses, passed her real estate licensing exam and went to work as a real estate agent. She started by selling homes, many in the secondary home market, on the lovely island she calls home, Brigantine.

By the end of year number one, Jean had won a silver medal for sales from the board of realtors. In her office, she was not only the "rookie of the year" but her sales totals topped the leader board among the 30 agents at Carrier and Associates, one of the area's biggest real estate firms. "When people asked me what I did that was so different, to make so many sales, I told them 'I was just being me' meaning I didn't lie and just went about my business of helping them find the right home," explains Jean. She looks for the customer's comfort zone and then finds what they want. "I don't try the used car salesman approach," adds Jean, whose honest, outgoing manner obviously works well.

"I love what I do," says Jean, who knows the value of hard work. "I'll be on the internet with a client answering questions at 4 A.M. if it's necessary to make a sale," she adds. In addition to being a people person, Jean knows the value of keeping up with technology. Her web site breaks down Brigantine into neighborhoods, describes the scenic island and, of course, includes listings. Unlike some other agents, Jean's web site is not all about her, but all about the area, including neighboring locations such as Atlantic City and Ocean City. "You need to always be one step ahead when it comes to technology and promoting yourself. There are over 100 agents on the (6.4 square mile) island alone, so if you don't promote yourself, you won't do well," adds Jean. She uses newspaper and magazine advertising to draw potential buyers to her web site at www. island-homesnj.com.

Next on Jean's timeline is to start on her quest for a broker's license. Then, down the road, her plans include possibly opening her own small real estate office with a couple of agents. For now, her plan is simply to be the best agent she can be—and that plan is working!

■ ■ ■

Getting ahead in the real estate field does not follow a typical career path. There are so many different possibilities, and yet, many real estate agents do not pursue them. In this chapter we look at several different approaches to getting ahead in real estate, including branching out, moving into different areas, or making a concerted effort to rise to the next level in your current career as an agent.

How to Excel in Real Estate and Move to the Next Level

There are several ways you can move to the next level, depending on what that next level means to you. For some, the next level means making more money by taking a new direction, whereas for others, it means making more money at what they currently do. Still others feel that there is a steady progression in their careers, and that moving up, such as from sales agent to broker, is the most direct way to progress and earn more money. Only you can determine what the next level means to you.

Before exploring the various ways to excel in the real estate industry, it is recommended that you join the National Association of Realtors (NAR). By joining your local real estate association, you are automatically extended membership in the state association and in the national association. To find out where the local board in your area is located, go to the NAR web site (www.realtor.org), which has a listing of the local associations. You can also look in your local phone directory or ask other agents, some of whom have probably joined. Although many people think that *real estate agent* is synonymous with *realtor* that is not technically the case. A *Realtor*® is a designated title for members of the NAR.

A benefit of joining the NAR, besides having access to more data through its web site and publications, is being able to take advantage of its ongoing education programs and special designations, which can lead you to the next level. Other organizations as well as many schools and universities also offer courses that can be advantageous. Continuing your education beyond required license renewal courses and gaining additional designations is typically a positive step in advancing any career, especially one with as many opportunities as real estate.

The following sections offer five suggestions that you can consider exploring as you move ahead in your real estate career.

Go into Commercial Real Estate

One way to move to another level of financial success is by venturing into commercial real estate. Walter Sanford, real estate coach, speaker, and entrepreneur, considers it a natural progression. By maintaining relationships with your residential clients, you are likely to become involved with their commercial real estate needs. Whether it is a natural progression or a conscious decision to take on commercial clients, you will need additional training and education in commercial real estate to succeed. There are some states where the same test is given for residential and commercial real estate licenses; in other states the exams are different. Either way, there is a lot to learn because commercial real estate includes industrial, retail, warehouses, apartment complexes, office parks, office buildings, restaurants, and even golf courses. Typically, commercial real estate agents find their niches and seek firms that handle that area.

Unlike residential real estate, there are fewer firms, and your choice is narrower once you have a specialty. However, your competition typically drops as well.

Major commercial firms want sellers with commercial experience, and according to Henry Munneke, who teaches commercial real estate at Terry Business College in Atlanta,

Georgia, commercial agents can often go 18 months to two years before making their first sale. Therefore, to start, people go into firms as analysts (which can mean many different things depending on the firms) or in to other jobs that support sales, such as research or marketing. Prudential Mortgage Capital, J.P. Morgan, and many other companies start newcomers in commercial real estate in such nonsales positions so that they can train for sales jobs.

Commercial real estate, in principle, is not unlike residential real estate, in that you are negotiating deals around the sale of property. However, the emotional aspect of home buying is replaced with the need for careful analysis of the potential growth for a business in a specific market. Numerous factors need to be incorporated into the equation when making a valuation and setting a price, including where the business is situated . . . hence the popular real estate phrase "location, location, location." Values are based on how well a business has fared in a given location, and how well the new location will support that business. Numerous factors are taken into account, and crunching numbers is part and parcel of commercial real estate.

While natural progression may lead you into commercial real estate, it is important to take the courses that teach you the many specifics of the field, to work in some capacity at such a firm, or even to apply to the real estate department of a major company. Franchise businesses, retail chains, hotels, and restaurants such as McDonald's, Target, and/ or Holiday Inn have real estate divisions scouting for new locations, analyzing the success of current franchises, and in some cases, closing down and selling off facilities in locations that are failing to generate sufficient revenue. Many people do not think about this end of commercial real estate. There are numerous possibilities, but like building a residential real estate business, it takes time to establish yourself. Having some money in the bank is important when making the transition into commercial real estate sales.

Become a Player

Another way to excel in real estate is to become a player. Many brokers, agents, developers, property managers, and others throughout the industry have taken the plunge themselves and bought property. Having learned how to value properties and analyze the market thoroughly, they utilize their abilities to know what to look for in a property and how to increase the value of that property.

Of course, the caveat to this method of forging ahead is that it takes money to make money. Therefore, you need to determine what you can afford to buy and how much more in expenses you can afford to take on. Often, if you can find a low-priced property in a growing market, you can buy it for a reasonable price, fix it up and rent it, which will provide a steady stream of income and pay for itself over time. As long as the real estate market continues to prosper in the area where you have purchased property, you can sell the property for a profit and purchase additional properties in the same or other growing markets.

Owning real estate can be extremely profitable, provided you can maintain the payments, upgrade and fix whatever needs repair, rent the property, or turn it over for a profit at the right time. You need to keep your finger on the pulse of the local real estate market.

This is a high risk/reward manner of making money in real estate. However, with due diligence on your part prior to buying, and by using what you have learned in the industry, you can shift the odds of success in your favor.

Often, people team up to go into real estate deals to ease the financial burden. It is highly advised that you be VERY careful with whom you partner. Friendships have been lost and relatives have stopped speaking to each other over such deals. Make sure you enter on relatively even financial ground and with very similar, if not identical, goals for the business. Make five- and ten-year plans, and stick to them.

Become a Real Estate Broker and Open Your Own Office

Being a broker does not assure you of more money. However, brokers nationwide have a median annual income nearly $20,000 more than that of agents. The key is opening an office in an area that is ripe with sales possibilities. An oversaturated market with a real estate office on every corner will not prove to be profitable. You need to open an office in a prime location and hire good sales agents to work for you.

The process of becoming a broker is not unlike that of becoming an agent, although it varies from state to state. You need to put in a certain number of hours of coursework and take a broker-licensing exam. Typically, you should have at least one or two years of experience as an agent before you become a broker. Having listed and sold properties, you will have a better idea of the different concerns that come up during real estate transactions and how to deal with such concerns or problems. The more you handle negotiations and find solutions for the glitches that occur, the more confident you will be that you can help sales agents solve their problems once you are a broker and open your own office.

Of course, opening an office typically means you will need to spend more money to make money. In the long run, however, a well-marketed, well-managed office can prove very fruitful. More on opening a real estate office can be found in Chapter 10.

Get a Designation

There are various designations that you can earn by taking additional courses. A designation by itself does not mean more money. However, along with such designations comes additional knowledge from having taken specialized courses.

A designation can give you an edge in a competitive field because it is often more attractive to potential clients who see that you have greater expertise. As a result, more listings and more customers will bring in more business. Of course, you need to use the designation as a marketing tool.

The Council of Residential Specialists, The National Association of Realtors, The Graduate Realtor Institute, and the National Association of Exclusive Buyer Agents are among the industry affiliated organizations and associations from which you can take courses to achieve designations. Designations include:

- Senior Real Estate Specialist (SRES)
- Accredited Buyer Representative (ABR)
- Certified Exclusive Buyer Agent (CEBA)
- Certified Buyer Representative (CBR)
- Accredited Land Consultant (ALC)
- Certified International Property Specialist (CIPS)
- Certified Property Manager (CPM)
- Counselor of Real Estate (CRE)

By exploring the web sites of the many real estate association and organizations, you can see what programs may be available and what designations interest you. Advanced courses from the NAR, for instance, include finance and investing, property management, land brokerage, and relocation. Various designations can be attained through taking these courses.

Be the Best at What You Do

Perhaps the most straightforward approach to moving to the next level is to focus on improving upon what you currently do. In real estate, you must treat your career as a business. This often means spending some money to make money. Taking additional classes, buying books, and attending seminars can help you learn the nuances of the business and find a system that works for you. Finding a mentor is also valuable, once you have been in the field for a few years and know where it is that you want your career to go.

Planning. It takes several steps to build a business, and you need to be highly motivated to surge forward from a comfortable level to one of greater success. First and foremost, you need to have a plan of action. How will you increase your contacts? Where will you farm for prospects? How much time will you allot for each of your primary tasks? The more detailed your plan of action, the less time you will waste spinning your wheels. Remember, you can use this and numerous other sources to list your duties. Also, keep in mind that you should utilize existing plans, strategies, and templates as guides so you do not try to re-create the wheel.

Next you need a schedule that encompasses not only your business life but also covers a portion of time for your nonbusiness life, including times with family and friends. You cannot sacrifice your personal life for your business, or you will eventually become resentful. Then both aspects of your life ultimately suffer. Make all of your scheduled time worthwhile, for business or for personal reasons. Because you are running your own business, you need not look busy for the sake of looking busy. Therefore, have everything planned out, from returning telephone calls and e-mails, to listing your properties, to following up with satisfied clients with whom you may not have spoken for some time.

Time efficiency. The two areas you will consistently need to focus on, if you really want to succeed in real estate, are seeking new business (prospecting), and getting rid of time wasters, that is, people who may never buy or sell. The first focus is simply being proactive. However, it is important that you continue to be proactive even if you have a busy schedule with sales totals climbing. You always need to be thinking about your future. Just as Sears and Macy's keep advertising even after their most profitable months, you always need to take time to look for new business. Do not stop and rest on your laurels.

The other half of this equation is more difficult. How can you tell the hot prospects from the duds? Remember, time is money, so the faster you get proficient at this aspect of the business—and it's not very easy, even for veteran agents—the faster you will spend more time making money and less time spinning your wheels. To motivate yourself to excel in this area, you should consider the amount of time it takes to show a couple 20 houses and then consider how much more quality time you could have spent with your family if you weren't doing the showings.

One of the factors that blurs the vision of some real estate agents is that they become emotionally involved. While you want to dedicate yourself to doing your best and should take your clients' wishes to heart, you should not dedicate such efforts to people who are essentially not concerned about your time and efforts. You need to be discerning and hold your emotions in check (at least until you believe that you are working with actual buyers and/or sellers).

To successfully differentiate between time wasters and actual buyers and sellers, you need to gather information quickly about the individuals involved. Why do they want to move? What is their motivation? Is something changing in the life of one, or all, of the people involved (such as a child on the way, a business relocating, or even a divorce)? Are they pre-approved buyers? Are they making any effort as sellers to make their home appealing to potential buyers? Are they looking toward the future or simply pondering the "what ifs"? The more you can put together a profile of your potential buyers and sellers, the more you can rid yourself of time wasters and build a business based on working closely with people who are forthright and looking to buy or sell a property.

Marketing. To be the best at what you do also entails marketing on your part. Marketing yourself in the modern era means having a good web site (see Figure 9.1), one that piques the interest of potential clients and leads them to taking action. Establishing yourself in your community—since that is where you are likely to do most of your business—is also important. McDonald's uses the Golden Arches. The early Century 21 employees all wore yellow jackets, and they were noticed. No, you do not need to do something with the color yellow, but you need to be omnipresent, so that the community knows that you are "the" local real estate agent or broker. You also need to join organizations, become a Realtor® by joining the NAR, and have your name and occupation included in local listings of associations.

FIGURE 9.1
Your Web Site

Everyone in business today has a web site, or so it seems. Nearly 70 percent of real estate agents have their own sites, and you should be among that group. Here is a quick overview of what you want to do when creating a web site.

1. Find a hosting service. Look at the major players, and go with one that provides good customer service (get references) at a decent price.

2. Search diligently for a good domain name. Try to include what you do in the domain name, such as JamesJonesRealEstate.com or HagerHomesales.com.

3. Have an inviting homepage that is NOT cluttered, but presents who you are and what you can do for a customer.

4. Provide quality content—people don't just want advertise-ments—have some lists, tips, or brief stories about real estate.

5. Think "they" not "you." Remember, it's about what the visitor can get from your web site, not all about what you've done in the past.

6. Limit detailed graphics and "hard-to-load" photos. If a page takes too long to load, you'll lose your visitors. Also, the glitzy web page is a thing of the past, except maybe for a casino web site.

7. Include a site map.

8. Include white space on the pages.

9. Include "Forward to a friend" around interesting content so that visitors can help you spread your name through viral marketing.

10. Maintain a consistent look and image from page to page—have a web designer who understands what YOU want. It's your page.

11. Use colors that complement one another and are easy to read. Remember that not everyone's monitor will represent colors the

same way. For this reason, many backgrounds remain white. Also odd colors can bleed or be very hard on the eyes.

12. Make sure your contact information appears on every page.

13. Make sure the site is easy to navigate, or "user friendly," meaning one or two clicks to get to where the visitor wants to be. Three clicks to find something is often like strike three, you're out.

14. Link to other types of real estate related businesses (such as a moving company or a business such as Lending Tree.com). This can be helpful for your clients.

15. Keep the site fresh with new updates and information.

16. Include keywords for search engine optimization. Don't just throw keywords around—use them in content and near the top of the page for best results on many search engines.

17. Be interactive—have a questionnaire or a survey for visitors to answer.

18. Make it easy to reach you, and respond to all e-mails within 24 hours.

19. Have your web site address on everything you use for marketing.

20. Regularly check that your links and pages work.

Finally, you need to be up-to-date technologically. This may mean hiring someone to install and educate you on the latest technology. Again, you have to spend some money to make money. The time it takes someone who is not techno-logically proficient to set up, learn, and use new technology correctly is wasted. It should also be noted: leaders in the field (any field) know when to ask for help.

Assistance. As you grow a real estate business, you may quickly find that there is more to do than you can handle. After all, you will be

- regularly prospecting for new clients.
- following up with potential clients.
- following up with previous clients.
- maintaining an up-to-date web site.
- preparing new listings and putting them on the MLS.
- servicing your current clients' needs.
- staying abreast of what is going on in the field.
- taking classes for license renewal and for your own benefit.
- attending local events and meetings of associations and organizations.
- handling office and administrative details.
- taking care of all paperwork, from disclosure forms to closing documents.
- trying to have a life outside of your career.

TEN TIPS FOR SUCCESS IN REAL ESTATE

1. Always know the territory in which you are buying or selling backwards and forwards.

2. Meet people in the industry, network constantly, and continue to build up your network. As real estate professor Henry Munneke says, "You never talk to a person without leaving with three names."

3. Always keep an open mind to new possibilities regarding jobs, sales, or any aspect of the business. It is a vast business, with opportunities you may know nothing about.

4. Look for someone who is where you would like to be in three, five, or ten years and try to set up an interview with her. You can learn a lot from people who are ahead of you in the same field.

5. Continue training and learning at all times.

6. Stay on top of new technology. People are becoming less and less forgiving if you do not know the newer programs.

7. Use due diligence as your ally. Always do your homework prior to meetings, closings, or any activities regarding specific properties.

8. Maintain contacts and remember to update your lists regularly. Contacts are key to success in real estate.

9. Know when to walk away from a sale, a deal, or even a job. Hone your skills at detecting a bad situation and weed out people who will waste your time.

10. Be proactive. Do not wait for leads, a new job, or anything to come to you in business. Go after what you want.

So you will eventually reach a point where you need to hire an assistant who has some knowledge of real estate. Carefully assess the skills of whomever you take on to help you, so they do not set you back. An assistant can handle office duties, filing, tracking the progress of listings, photographing homes for virtual tours, updating the web site, organizing the paperwork you need for each client, and handling phones, e-mails, and other communications. A good assistant can essentially free up your time to focus on clients—servicing them and finding new ones. Consider interns as a possibility. Also note that the NAR has courses that certify assistants. Contact the local NAR or go to www.realtor.org for information on finding a certified assistant in your area.

To be the best in any field means finding a competitive edge, what makes you different than your competition. This means becoming known in the industry for your specific abilities, studying the industry very carefully, and finding a niche. Titles and designations notwithstanding, becoming a top producer *is* what the next level is all about for many real estate agents, and it takes great motivation and dedication.

Using Timelines and Benchmarks to Keep Your Career on Track

If you are serious about making progress in your career, you can set benchmarks as guideposts. You may want to start by motivating yourself to have X number of listings and X number of sales at the end of two years, three years, and five years. Your plan may then be to go for your broker's license at night.

The idea of setting up timelines and benchmarks is to realistically set a framework for your future. The 23-year-old former intern, David Fischer mentioned in Chapter 7, is now working at Bank of America in its real estate finance division. However, he and his brother plan to grow their own real estate business by purchasing two properties a year over the next five years and then, by using the rent from the properties, pay down the mortgages as fast as possible so that they can then fix-up and sell the properties for a profit. They have devised their own timeline and set benchmarks for where they anticipate their business will be in five and ten years. Likewise, because you are essentially running your own real estate business as an independent contractor, you should devise realistic five- and ten-year plans, including how much you anticipate listing and selling, along with when you plan to return to school for designations or other advanced education.

Timelines, benchmarks, and five- and ten-year plans are useless if you don't refer to them. Review your plan every few months and see how your progress measures up. While you will not necessarily stay 100 percent on track, the closer you stick to your plans, the more confident you will be that you are moving forward on your career path.

CHAPTER 10

Opening Your Own
Real Estate Office

PROFILE

Beverly Fairchild

Agent Turned Co-Owner

Beverly Fairchild started out in the interior design business. She opted for real estate when her daughter was in kindergarten, choosing a career that was still close to her design interests but also one that would afford her a more flexible schedule, allowing her to be around her family more. Through a contact, she was able to become sponsored by the local Century 21 office and then took courses and passed the test for her real estate license. Once licensed, she became an agent at a nearby Century 21 location in Connecticut.

From the start, Beverly made an effort to become as educated as possible, taking classes and attending seminars in hopes of being on top of as many aspects of the business as she could. "If there are courses or seminars offered and you don't take advantage of the opportunities to learn, you're cutting off your nose to spite your face," says Fairchild, who not only established herself as a local agent, but later went on to get her broker's license. Two years ago, after nearly 14 years at Century 21, she teamed with a friend in the business. Together they opened, or in this case reopened, a business called Collins-Morrow Real Estate, which handled residential properties in the New Fairfield and Sherman areas of Connecticut.

Collins-Morrow had been a highly successful real estate business in the area since the 1950s. The business had evolved into a major development company for a number of years, and many of the properties in the region were developed by Collins-Morrow. It wasn't until the early 1990s that the business became inactive, as undeveloped property was nearly impossible to find.

It was Renee Collins, wife of one former partner, who teamed with Beverly Fairchild to relaunch the business in 2003. Together they set out to take what had become an inactive real estate company and bring it back to prominence. When Renee and Beverly reopened Collins-Morrow, it immediately drew attention. "People knew the name and responded to it," says Collins. "It was a name that had been passed down through generations of homeowners in the area, who had either bought or sold Collins-Morrow properties over the previous 50 years."

Together they built on the history of the business and provided first-rate customer service "We're very compassionate with the needs of the people we work with," explains Fairchild. "We're wives, we're daughters, we're mothers . . . we've run the full gamut. We know what it's like to have that scary, uneasy feeling buying your first house or what's on the mind of a family with children looking to buy a new home. We understand the needs of the family with elderly parents. We have a wealth of both real life and real estate experience, particularly in this area."

Collins-Morrow handles a wide range of housing, including condos, co-ops, newly constructed homes, and waterfront properties. "We also handle equestrian properties and even a gated golf community," says Collins, referring to their niche markets.

Today, the women serve 26 towns, and using their knowledge, compassion, and industry know-how, Renee Collins and Beverly Fairchild have created a highly successful real estate business.

■   ■   ■

It is certainly not something you will do early in your real estate career, but at some point, after you have established yourself and learned about the business, you may wish to open your own real estate office. To do so, you need to take the classes for your broker's exam and become licensed. As a licensed broker, you can have agents work for you as independent contractors, much the way you worked as an agent for someone else. It is important, however, to remember that as a broker you become responsible for these agents and their headaches become your headaches.

Opening an office of your own requires you to

- find a good location, one in which you can grab a share of the market.
- be available, or on call, 24/7.
- procure funding.
- assume fiduciary responsibility for all deals made through your office.
- handle all financial matters including maintaining a budget.
- find good agents.
- provide training.
- hire support staff.
- establish yourself in the community through marketing.
- do your own advertising.
- establish your ground rules and business policies.

Starting any business, real estate or not, requires planning, funding, projections for the future, and a tremendous amount of time and dedication. To help all of these aspects fall into place smoothly, it is highly recommended that you begin with a realistic, well-prepared business plan. A business plan is often the means by which entrepreneurs obtain financial backing. It is also the way business owners carefully put all of their plans and ideas into one document they can follow during their start-up phase and can use to monitor their businesses over time.

Starting with a Business Plan

While no two business plans will be the same, there are many guiding principles that you can follow. It is to your benefit to use the wisdom of those who have come before you by looking at other business plans and using the structure that others have used. Before starting on your business plan, however, establish the goals and objectives of your company. Therefore, you should ask yourself several key questions:

- What will be my market? Residential? Private homes? Apartments? Commercial? Both?
- What area, neighborhood, or region should I cover?
- Will I handle niche or specialty markets? Which ones should I go after?
- What are my areas of strength, and how can I utilize them in this business endeavor?
- How large an office do I need?
- How many agents should I start with?
- How much support staff will I need?

- How will I compete with existing firms?
- Should I open an office independently or buy a franchise?

The answers to these questions will be the starting point from which you can launch a business.

To start the business plan, you need to have a vision of where you see the company going in the future. This does not mean that in the ever-changing real estate market you won't be changing along with it. Companies and their business plans should always be works in progress. They should be created with the flexibility to adapt to change. New technology, changing real estate laws, the economy, and other factors make it imperative that you are open to change as your business progresses. The inflexible business usually goes the way of the dinosaur.

The Business Plan

The following is an outline for your business plan. But, also look for templates on web sites and in books that focus on creating these important blueprints for success.

The Table of Contents (TOC)

It may not sound very important, but the TOC will make life a lot easier for you and others reading your document or looking for key information. Keep it simple, straightforward, and no longer than one page. There is no definite right or wrong way to number the sections of your business plan.

Some plans have 1.0, 1.1, 1.2 defining subsections within each section, whereas others have 1a, 1b, 1c. The choice is yours; just be consistent.

The Executive Summary

The executive summary is the most important part of the business plan. It is typically a one- or two-page general summary of the business including the who, what, when, where, and why of the business. A subsection will include your future objectives. For example, you might say that XYZ Real Estate will open in such and such neighborhood, be owned by yourself as a licensed real estate broker, and have three licensed real estate agents handing residential properties in a defined area. You can then mention, in a paragraph, why you chose this location, noting the benefits.

Along with being profitable, your objectives may be to expand to a larger market, to add more agents, to provide real estate training programs, to become known in the community, be the leading company in a particular area, perhaps in a niche market, to make money (commissions from sales), and so on. Be realistic, but plan for your future and briefly describe the overall plan in this section. You can then explain, briefly, how you can make these goals a reality by emphasizing your strengths and knowledge of both the overall real estate market and the area you will be covering. Try to be concise in your executive summary because you will go into greater detail as you proceed.

Note: Although it is at the beginning of the document, often the executive summary is written last, after you've made various determinations in the specific sections of the plan. Also, if written first, this section tends to be way too long and turns into a novel. Therefore, consider doing everything else and then summarizing all of your work in this section—hence, the word *summary*.

Industry Analysis

Depending on who is going to be reading your business plan, you may or may not include an industry analysis. If you do, you should discuss the real estate industry first in broad terms and then in terms of your slice of the pie, your area of coverage. You can discuss the latest changes within the industry and provide an overview of how you will utilize the new information and/or new technological advantages. This section shows that you are on top of the industry, aware of what is going on in your segment of that industry, and have a plan for utilizing that which is helping to drive the industry forward to your advantage. If you are looking for backers, include some statistics to illustrate that this is a thriving industry.

Business Overview or Company Summary

Call it what you choose, but in this section you need to provide a comprehensive description of your plans (within a few pages). Start off with the legal structure (LLC, partnership, sole proprietorship), and proceed to include your goals and objectives for the business. Then provide the details. Answering the following questions should help:

- Where will you be located?
- How will the business operate?
- How many people do you foresee working in your office?
- What type of record keeping will you be using?
- How will you generate leads?
- What documentation will sellers sign? Buyers?
- How will you determine who handles new clients?
- What kind of training will you provide?
- What niche will you fill, if any?
- Who is your target audience? Buyers? Sellers? Both?
- Do you have a business philosophy?
- What technology hardware and software will you use?
- What will you provide for agents, and what will they need to pay for themselves?

This section provides the key selling points, or strengths, of your business, along with the broad details of your complete plan.

Services

Here you want to outline what specific services you can provide for sellers and for buyers. For example, for sellers you might discuss providing them with a free comparative market analysis, for buyers the possibility of a visual tour, local advertisements, an open house, flyers or brochures and so on. For sellers, detail what you can do that goes above and beyond expectations to sell their homes at good prices. For buyers, include the ways which you will seek out the properties that best match their needs and criteria. For example, you might have them fill out questionnaires, do special computer searches on their behalf, show them virtual tours, and so on. You should also address the services you will provide for agents to draw them to your business and to retain them in a competitive field in which other firms may try recruiting them.

Marketing Plan or Marketing Summary

This is an important section because it is where you define your target market. It is hard to have inventory to meet all needs. Therefore, in residential real estate you may have private homes and townhouses, but not condos or co-ops. In commercial real estate you may very likely specialize and target a specific market, such as shopping malls and retailers whose businesses fit well in the malls.

Along with defining your target market, you want to explain how you intend to capture a percentage of that market. For example, if you are representing several retirement communities as one of your primary niche markets, how will you best reach the over-60 demographic audience looking to buy into such a community? How you reach the demographic target group is important.

Whatever audience you want to reach, be it sellers, buyers, a combination of both, or a niche group within the categories, you have to determine whether you will focus your attention on marketing yourself through the local print media, by presentations or literature at neighborhood activities, on the internet, or on local radio or television. Discuss the means by which you will spread the word through marketing and advertising to let it be known that you are in business. You should also do a cost breakdown. How much will it cost you to market to your target group?

Competitive Analysis

When looking for financial backers, attracting top agents, and to provide yourself with a competitive edge, you want to develop a competitive analysis. This is the section in which you discuss the competition. To do this adequately, you need to do some investigative research, which may mean posing as a buyer and visiting open houses, surfing the web for your competitors' sites, or calling an agent in a competitor's office. Get as much information as possible on other local firms. Determine their strengths and weaknesses. You want to include all the basic facts about the top competitors in your region or area and then include analysis of indirect competition that may come from national companies that aren't necessarily based nearby.

Next, you want to carefully determine what you can do that your competition is not doing. Can you provide a service that is not being provided elsewhere in your area? Show what you can do that will give you a leg up on the competition, that "competitive edge." This can be the single most important section of your business plan. Make it clear that you are prepared to carve out your own segment of the market and provide details regarding how you propose to do it.

Operations Plan

This is sometimes included in the business summary. It is a more detailed overview of how the day-to-day business activities will take place. Each business has its own methods of operation. Are there forms to fill out as soon as someone comes into your firm? Does someone greet each new client and introduce him to an agent on floor duty? How will your business work? Walk the reader through a typical day in your office. Discuss how many agents she will find and how much support is on hand for the agents and for the clients. How, when, and where are training classes given? Is there a separate location? How are open houses handled? How are ads placed, and by whom? This is a way of detailing the activities of the business. You can be broad or detailed in this section depending on who the reader will be.

Management Team

You will need to include a paragraph or two on the key players, which may only be yourself. The person behind the business is

VERY important, especially if you are looking for outside funding. Therefore, a concise three or four paragraph bio that sings your praises is beneficial. Stay focused on activities that relate to your real estate and/or business skills. Include your sphere of influence, or some information about how well connected you are, because that is a very important aspect of building this kind of a business.

Financial Plan

Numbers, numbers, and more numbers. Again, the level of detail will depend on your purpose for writing the plan and who will be reading it. If the plan is written to acquire funding, you will need to provide all of the possible financial information in greater detail than if this were a plan for you alone to follow.

Either way, you will want to include where your profits will come from. This includes commissions and how they will be calculated. Also include where you will spend money. Training? Office supplies and technology? Advertising? Include all projected income and expenditures. Be realistic, especially when projecting profits three, five, seven, and ten years in the future. Although you won't know what the market will be, you can determine how much it will cost you to grow from a firm with four agents to one with 14, how many sales you can anticipate per year based on a past history of local sales in the area, and at what prices homes will be sold. Be conservative.

Explain on what general assumptions you are basing your financial projections. For example, you will probably assume that the real estate industry remains at least where it is currently. In short, always include a paragraph on how you are getting your numbers.

Among the financial documents you should include are

- Break-even analysis
- Projected profit and loss statement
- Projected cash flow
- Projected balance sheet

If you are seeking funding from other sources, let it be known where your other funding will be coming from. Most often, anyone providing you with a loan does not want to think that he is your only source of funding. In addition, it is common for most start-ups to be funded in large part by the principle owner—you. It's much easier to get a loan from an established lender if it sees that you are also putting a significant sum of money into your business.

Projected sales, operating expenses, and profit margin are also important to include in the business plan. They can also be used as indicators so you will know when you have reached projected milestones.

Staffing

Staffing in a real estate office is a combination of hiring support staff that understands real estate and meets the needs of the agents working in the office as well as the clients. Duties can range from answering phones and sitting at the front desk to doing research and assisting in various other office matters. Before hiring support staff, make a detailed list of staff responsibilities and how many you can afford to hire. Also consider some interns, but not too many. Determine ahead of time, rules and guidelines for office personnel. Look for professionalism, experience, people skills, research ability, honesty, and ethics as important qualities in whomever you hire.

The key to running a successful real estate office is recruiting quality agents. Good agents mean more business, more profits, and a strong reputation. It is important to look for agents who rank customer service and satisfaction at the top of their lists. The days of making a sale by telling customers anything they wanted to hear are long gone. Today's customers are savvy, and agents must be honest, ethical, and ready to go the extra mile for a good customer. Referrals are very important in the real estate industry and that is in direct correlation to first-rate customer service.

The level of experience is important because training will cost you time and money. However, experience on paper is not as valuable as the agent's desire to learn and continue building his skills. Therefore, the agent who is looking to sit back and coast on her 20 years in the business may not be what you are looking for. Instead, the hungry, young, up-and-comer with three years experience may have new angles for lead generation, and systems that may work wonders. Be open to new as well as more experienced agents.

Once you are actively seeking new agents, you need to prepare your own office policies prior to interviews. Commissions, fees, and all parameters and guidelines need to be in place. First, determine what money you have to spend and then determine which expenses you will pay and which expenses will be the responsibility of the agents. Will you provide a web page for each agent? Who will handle advertising? You need to make a list and clearly decide who will pay what and how much you can afford to spend in order to make money.

Ask what technology and software programs they have experience using. Their database and spheres of influence are as important as their strategies and philosophies. Certification and specialties may be valuable to your firm, so ask them about these areas. Get a feel for the integrity of the individual. Will he conduct himself in a way that will inspire confidance in your company?

Finally, meet with agents who, are interviewing you while you are interviewing them.

Franchises

A different approach to starting a real estate business is opening up a franchise. Several of the national and international industry giants, such as Century 21, are franchises. Most franchise companies have succeeded by starting their businesses and in turn selling franchises to new entrepreneurs looking to open a business. Century 21, however, got off the ground in a unique manner; they bought up existing businesses, which then became franchises.

Only you can decide whether converting your existing business or starting out as a franchisee is better for you than being an independent business owner. Becoming a franchise owner affords you much greater leverage when it comes to marketing and advertising. It can also give you more buying power, greater training capabilities, and access to tried and true systems.

Of course, the two negative factors of franchising are the fees you pay to the franchise company and the loss of freedom. Paying fees to the franchise company is less of a factor if you do the math and determine that with the additional advertising and the well-known company name, your sales will be up significantly. Of course, you may only know this if you try starting out on your own first. As for "freedom," it is only to your benefit if you have strategies and plans that are profitable and not in line with what the franchise company uses as a business policy. For example, if you have a specialized niche market and you can benefit by working in your geographic region in a manner that is area specific, you might be better off as an independent business owner than following the format implemented by the franchise company. A real estate firm specializing in historic houses might find that its unique niche doesn't benefit by following franchise guidelines, nor is it in direct competition with the mainstream franchises.

FRANCHISE START-UP COSTS

The cost to purchase and start up a franchise varies greatly between franchise companies and even within a company because of location, area served, and size of the office. For example, a Century 21 Real Estate, LLC could run from around $20,000 to over $500,000; Coldwell Banker, would typically be in the range of $20,000 to $70,000; ReMAX from $20,000 to $200,000 and Weichert Real Estate Affiliates Inc. from $45,000 to $254,000.

Unlike fast food franchises, where there is always more food to be delivered, you have a finite number of properties in your market, or markets. If you can represent a large share of the market without franchising, then you will do just fine. Perhaps you have been in an industry where you built up a following in the neighborhood. People may know and trust you already, so you won't need big advertising dollars to go out and reach them.

However, if you are in a market that already has other franchises, and you are trying to establish yourself without a specialized niche or a means of taking a large market share from the start, you might be better off with the big company behind you.

Marketing, contacts, business experience, your ability to recruit top agents to work for you, your overall sphere of influence, and size of the area you are covering are all factors that need to be considered along with the projected bottom line.

Lastly, determine if you are the franchise type or the independent entrepreneurial type. Do you feel comfortable handling all aspects of the business on your own? Do you feel locked in when using someone else's system? How much risk are you comfortable taking?

Both franchises and independent real estate companies have been, and can be, very successful. Once you are ready to open your own business, you need to make the call.

Before starting a real estate business, make sure you are comfortable taking on greater responsibility and are ready to handle financial burdens until the business takes off. Just as starting out as a new agent means having some funds available, opening a business means having greater funding available to get the business through the early start-up period, which, depending on the region and the agents in your stable, could be months or years.

Buying an Established Real Estate Firm

There is also the option of buying an established real estate business, which affords you local name recognition and reputation while saving you many of the start-up woes. Of course, when buying a business, you need to do a great deal of research to make sure that you are not acquiring great debt, legal hassles, or other problems. Negotiating the contract carefully with an attorney will help you determine whether or not the business is carrying debt.

Beyond the past data available on a business you are looking to buy, you need to assess the value of the business and compare that with the price the seller is asking. Of course, your real estate experience will prove helpful in this regard. However, unlike a physical property, such as a building or a house, there are intellectual properties, experience, and the name recognition factored into the sales price. How much did someone's skills and abilities play a part in the success of the business? Does the company have a system that works, and how much is that worth to you? Is its name well known? All of this needs to be factored into the sales equation, along with what you can bring to this business that you believe can help make it grow. You need to look at the future and determine whether or not the seller is getting out at the right time or this business can, and will, continue or prosper under your guidance.

Resources

Organizations and Associations

American Homeowners Association (AHA)®
P.O. Box 16817
Stamford, CT 06905
Phone: (800) 470-2242 or (203) 323-7715
www.ahahome.com

American Land Title Association
1828 L Street NW
Washington, DC 20036-5104
Phone: (800) 787-ALTA/Fax (888) FAX-ALTA
www.alta.org

American Seniors Housing Association
5100 Wisconsin Avenue NW, Suite 307

Washington, DC 20016
Phone: (202) 237-0900/Fax: (202) 237-1616
www.seniorhousing.org

American Society of Appraisers

555 Herndon Parkway, Suite 125
Herndon, VA 20170
Phone: (703) 478-2228/Fax: (703) 742-8471
www.appraisers.org
e-mail: asainfo@appraisers.org

American Society of Home Inspectors® Inc.

932 Lee Street, Suite 101
Des Plaines, IL 60016
Phone: (800) 743-2744 or (847) 759-2820/Fax (847) 759-1620
www.ashi.org

Association of Commercial Real Estate

2400 22nd Street, Suite 110
Sacramento, CA 95818
Phone: (916) 446-0775/Fax: (916) 451-9150
www.acre.org

Building Owners and Managers Association (BOMA)

1201 New York Avenue NW, Suite 300
Washington, DC 20005
Phone: (202) 408-2662/Fax: (202) 371-0181
www.boma.org
e-mail: info@boma.org

Counsel of Real Estate Brokerage Managers

430 North Michigan Avenue

Chicago, IL 60611

Phone: (800) 621-8738/Fax: (312) 329-8882

www.crb.com

e-mail: info@crb.com

Council of Residential Specialists

430 North Michigan Avenue, 3rd Floor

Chicago, IL 60611

Phone: (800) 462-8841/Fax: (312) 329-8551

www.crs.com

e-mail: crshelp@crs.com

Fannie Mae

3900 Wisconsin Avenue NW

Washington, DC 20016-2892

Phone: (202) 752-7000

www.fanniemae.com/headquarters@fanniemae.com

Freddie Mac

8200 Jones Branch Drive

McLean, VA 22102-3110

Phone: (703) 903-2000

www.freddiemac.com

Institute of Real Estate Management (IREM)

430 North Michigan Avenue

Chicago, IL 60611

Phone: (312) 329-6067/Fax: (312) 410-7967

www.irem.org

International Council of Shopping Centers

1221 Avenue of the Americas, 41st Floor

New York, NY 10020-1099

Phone: (646) 728-3800/Fax (732) 694-1755

www.icsc.org

e-mail: icsc@icsc.org

Mortgage Bankers Association of America

1919 Pennsylvania Avenue NW

Washington, DC 20006-3404

Phone: (202) 557-2700

www.mbaa.org

National Association of Home Builders

1201 15th Street NW

Washington, DC 20005

Phone: (800) 368-5242 or (202) 266-8200

Fax: (202) 266-8400

www.homebuilder.com

National Association of Independent
Real Estate Brokers

7102 Mardyke Lane

Indianapolis, IN 46226

Phone: (317) 549-1709, ext. 133

www.nationalrealestatebrokers.org

e-mail: director@nationalrealestatebrokers.org

National Association of Industrial and Office Properties

2001 Cooperative Way, 3rd Floor
Herndon, VA 20171-3034
Phone: (703) 904-7100/Fax: (703) 904-7942
www.naiop.org

National Association of Review Appraisers and Mortgage Underwriters

1224 North Nokomis NE
Alexandria, MN 56308
Phone: (320) 763-6870/Fax: (320) 763-9290
www.iami.org/nara
e-mail: nara@iami.org

National Association of Realtors® (NAR)

430 North Michigan Avenue
Chicago, IL 60611-4087

Washington, DC Office
500 New Jersey Avenue NW
Washington, DC 20001-2020
Phone: (800) 874-6500
www.realtor.com or www.realtor.org

National Association of Residential Property Managers (NARPM) Headquarters

184 Business Park Drive, Suite 200–P
Virginia Beach, VA 23462
Phone: (800) 782-3452/Fax: (866) 466-2776

www.narpm.org
e-mail: info@narpm.org

National Trust for Historic Preservation

1785 Massachusetts Avenue NW
Washington, DC 20036-2117
Phone: (202) 588-6000/Fax: (202) 588-6038
www.nationaltrust.org

The Real Estate Educators Association

9 Mantua Road
Mt. Royal, NJ 08061
Phone: (856) 423-3215/Fax: (856) 423-3420
www.reea.org
e-mail info @reea.org

United States Department of Housing and Urban Development (HUD)

451 7th Street SW
Washington, DC 20410
Phone: (202) 708-1112/TTY: (202) 708-1455
www.hud.gov

Women's Council of REALTORS®

430 North Michigan Avenue
Chicago, IL 60611
www.wcr.org
e-mail: info @wcr.org

Books

There are numerous real estate books available. The key is to find those that are relatively current (2000 or later) and in line with your goals. Avoid the get-rich-quick books and focus on those you believe can help you in your career. Below are a few of the many titles for agents and brokers.

Bowman, John L., *How to Succeed in Commercial Real Estate* (Mesa House Publishing, 2004).

Cook, Frank, *21 Things I Wish My Broker Had Told Me: Practical Advice for New Real Estate Professionals* (Dearborn Real Estate Education, 2002).

Cross, Carla, *Up and Running in 30 Days: A Proven Plan for Financial Success in Real Estate* (Dearborn Real Estate Education, 2001).

Davis, Darryl, *How to Become a Power Agent in Real Estate: A Top Industry Trainer Explains How to Double Your Income in 12 Months* (McGraw Hill, 2002).

Dick, James, and J.W. Dicks, *How to Buy and Sell Real Estate for Financial Freedom* (McGraw-Hill, 2006).

Edwards, Kenneth W., *Your Successful Real Estate Career, 4th edition* (American Management Association, 2003).

Klein, Saul D., John W. Reilly, Michael Barnett, *Real Estate Technology Guide* (Dearborn Real Estate Education, 2003).

Martin, Joseph H., *Real Estate License Examinations: A Complete Guide to Salesperson, Broker, and Appraisal Exams, 5th edition* (Arco Professional Certification and Licensing Examination Series, Peterson's Guides, 2002).

McCrea, Bridget, *Real Estate Agent's Field Guide: The Essential Insider Advice for Surviving in a Competitive Market* (AMACOM, 2004).

Morgan, Wayne, and Lynn Morgan, *How to Get Rich in Real Estate, and Have a Life!* (Authorhouse, 2004).

Real Estate Sourcebook (Reed Publishing).

Sanford, Walter, *Sanford's Stellar Checklists* (Sanford Systems, 2005).

Sullivan, Marilyn, *Complete Idiot's Guide to Success as a Real Estate Agent* (Alpha, 2003).

Yoegel, John A., *Real Estate License Exams For Dummies* (For Dummies, 2005).

Zeller, Dirk, *Your First Year in Real Estate: Making the Transition from Total Novice to Successful Professional* (Three Rivers Press, 2001).

Web Sites

The major real estate organizations and associations all have web sites. You will also find that looking at the sites of major firms can be beneficial. Here are a few places to get started.

www.360house.com: Virtual home tour service

www.Access2Re.com: Services for real estate professionals

www.AtValue.com: Real estate software

www.BarryInc.com: Nationwide real estate services for professionals

www.Biztrader.com: Online commercial property classifieds

www.CBRE.com: Market research from CB Richard Ellis

www.Century21.com: Comprehensive site from leading national firm

www.Coldwellbanker.com: Residential listings site

www.Coldwellbankercommercial.com: Commercial listings site

www.ColdwellProperty.com: Comprehensive site from leading national firm

www.Colliers.com: Market research from Colliers International

www.Commrex.com: Lead generation, listings, mortgages, financing, and research

www.CoStar.com: Market research: office buildings and industrial properties

www.Cushwake.com: Cushman and Wakefield's comprehensive site

www.DataQuick.com: Comprehensive nationwide data research site www.DealMover.com: Online transaction management

www.Dttus.com: Deloitte and Touche real estate data, research, and services

www.eREI.com: Data integration, data mining, analytics, and GIS for commercial real estate industry

www.e-Space.com: Online commercial solutions provider

www.EY.com: Research and consulting site from Ernst &Young

www.ForSaleByOwner.com: Fee-based national listings of homes for sale by owner

www.FreeForeclosureSearch.com: National listing of fore-closed properties

www.Homesalez.com: For sale by owner listings

www.Homeservices.com: Portal of brokers/agents

www.LoopNet.com: Major commercial property listings site

www.LotsUSA.com: National listing of real estate lots for sale

www.NewHomes.com: Nationwide co-op broker listings of new homes for sale

www.Number1Expert.com: Link to over 2,000 popular real estate sites

www.Pikenet.com: International real estate portal

www.PropertyRover.com: Commercial information provider and property search engine www.Prudential.com: Comprehensive site from leading national firm

www.RealData.com: Real estate software

www.RealDataExchange.com: Real estate portal

www.RealEstate.com: Lending Tree's comprehensive real estate site

http://RealEstate.yahoo.com: Real estate resources

www.RealEstateBrokerage.com: National commercial real estate firm and 1031 exchanges site

www.RealEstateZoo.com: Commercial real estate portal

www.RealHound.com: Market research software

www.Realtor.com: Information from the National Association of Realtors

www.Realty.com: Large real estate resource portal

www.RealtyLocator.com: The latest real estate news stories plus 100,000 real estate links

www.Rebuz.com: Real estate industry portal

www.ReLibrary.com: Real estate portal

www.Remax.com: Comprehensive site from leading national firm

www.Reri.com: Real Estate Research Institute's site

www.Risco.net: MLS and other technology for Realtors®

www.Sitelink.com: Catylist-CCIMNet's technology site for real estate professionals

www.TWR.com: Torto Wheatron Research for commercial, industrial, and residential properties

www.Yardi.com: Real estate software

Glossary

Adjustable Rate Mortgage (ARM). A mortgage loan that reflects changes in interest rates. Monthly payments increase or decrease at intervals predetermined by the lender. There are a wide variety of these loans, and there is usually a cap on how much the interest amount can change.

Amenity. A nonessential feature, such as a swimming pool or hardwood floors in a home that increases the value of the property.

Amortization. The repayment of a mortgage loan through monthly payments of principal and interest that follow a set schedule and lead to the ownership of the property in a specific number of years.

Appraisal. An estimate of the fair market value of a property. It should be made by a licensed appraiser.

Balloon mortgage. A type of mortgage that usually has low rates for a specified time period, after which the payments balloon to much higher rates.

Borrower. The individual who receives a loan from a lender. The borrower is obligated to repay the loan, along with any additional fees, in a specified period of time.

Broker. In real estate, a broker is state licensed and can represent buyers and/or sellers in a real estate transaction. Brokers can open offices. They then assume the fiduciary responsibility of any agents who work for them.

Building code. The regulations under which safety standards are upheld for a building. Usually such codes specify the materials that can be used in construction and repairs, as well as fire and safety measures.

Buyer-agency agreement. Newer, and less common than seller agreements, a buyer agreement establishes a formal relationship between a buyer and an agent for a specified time period. In such agreement, the agent will include what he intends to do on behalf of a client in exchange for exclusive rights to represent that client in the real estate buying market. Some states mandate that such an agreement be signed.

Buyer's agent. In a real estate transaction, a buyer's agent represents the best interests of the buyer. The agent is responsible for disclosing all information she knows about the property to her clients and negotiating fairly on behalf of all clients.

Certificate of title. A certificate validating that a property legally belongs to the owner. Such a certificate is often provided by a title company.

Closing. The formal transfer of ownership of property from the seller to the buyer takes place when all final paperwork is signed, payments are settled, and the title is transferred to the buyer.

Closing costs. The various fees and costs, beyond the sale price of the property, that are paid at the closing, which may include points, title insurance, document fees, prepaid interest, and property taxes.

Closing statement. A document detailing the payments made during the real estate closing process.

Commission. The percentage paid to the agent or broker for her part in the real estate transaction.

Condominium. Units of a larger property, such as an apartment building, that are sold to individual owners who typically share financial responsibility for common areas. However, the owners own their individual units outright and are free to sell when they choose to whomever they choose.

Cooperative (co-op). A multifamily structure, such as an apartment building, in which owners buy units within the overall property as shareholders. A co-op board makes the decisions for the property, and owners pay maintenance fees for the upkeep of the property and their units. Board members vote on new buyers.

Credit report. A document that lists the past credit history of the individual(s), including timeliness of paying bills and repaying loans.

Deed. A document used to indicate the ownership of a property and transfer of such ownership.

Discount point. Also known as "points," these are payments made to decrease the overall principal amount of the loan. Points may be requested by the lender to lessen the risk on the loan, or they may be paid by the borrower to lower his debt. Each point is equal to 1 percent of the total loan amount.

Down payment. An upfront payment of a percentage of the overall purchase price of the property. Most real estate transactions include some down payment by the buyers.

Dual agency. An agent who acts on behalf of both the seller and the buyer. This is illegal in some states and highly unethical unless both parties are aware of the situation and agree to it.

Equity. The amount of ownership the owner has in the property. It is based on how much of the mortgage she has paid off to that point.

Fair Housing Act (FHA). Passed in 1968, the FHA prohibits discrimination against homebuyers on the basis of race, religion, sex, nationality, family status, or disability.

Federal Housing Administration (FHA). Established in 1934, the FHA provides lenders with mortgage insurance in the event a borrower defaults on the loan. This allows lenders to take greater risks and, in turn, broadens the number of potential homebuyers by making it easier for people to obtain loans.

Fiduciary. Someone who is entrusted to act responsibly and in the best interests when handling the property or investments of another party.

Fixed-rate mortgage. A mortgage in which interest payments are set at a specified rate and do not change during the life of the loan.

Foreclosure. The process in which a property is sold legally, to pay the loan of the lender because a borrower has defaulted.

Full disclosure. In real estate, this pertains to providing all knowledge and information an individual has about a specific property.

Good faith estimate. A document provided to the borrower by the lender that carefully estimates the costs to the borrower, including all prepaid escrow items plus closing fees and costs.

Homeowners' association. A group of homeowners who unite, often setting up guidelines and organizing activities for the betterment of the community.

Homeowner's insurance. An insurance policy for homeowners, providing protection against damage to the property and against claims made because of accidents incurred on the property.

Inspections. Typically, inspections are made to find and disclose defects or problems within the property that could affect the safety of individuals and/or the resale value of the property. Various types of inspection will uncover specific problems that need to be addressed prior to a sale.

Interest. A charge made by a lender for borrowing money, based on a percentage of the loan amount.

Inventory. In real estate, inventory is typically the number of properties for rent or for sale.

Lease. An agreement, usually contractual, in which the owner of a property allows a lessee, or tenant, to rent the property or a portion thereof for a specified time period. Provisions regarding the use of the property, necessary repairs, and maintenance are usually included in the lease.

Listing agreement. An agreement between the seller of the property and the licensed representative (broker) who will be employed to sell the property. Such an agreement includes a finite time in which the seller's representative may use her best efforts to find a buyer for the property and the commission the representative will receive if a sale is made.

Lockbox. A commonly used devise that attaches to the door of a property and holds the key in a secure manner so that agents can show the property.

Market value. The "standard" price a property would probably generate if sold on the open market.

Mortgage. A loan established by a lender to pay for the property over a certain amount of time.

Mortgage banker. A company that originates loans and resells them to secondary mortgage lenders like Fannie Mae or Freddie Mac.

Mortgage broker. An agent that brings a borrower and lender together for the sake of a mortgage agreement.

Mortgage insurance. Insurance policy that protects lenders in the event the borrower cannot pay the mortgage loan. Typically, this is required if a homeowner cannot provide a down payment of at least 20 percent of the cost of the property.

Multiple Listing Service (MLS). A service that list homes for sale or rent, usually computerized. It affords brokers the opportunity to share their listings with other real estate professionals.

Noncompete clause. A clause in a lease (in commercial real estate) that prevents the leaser from leasing to a similar or competing business within a specific area, such as in the same shopping mall.

Open house. A set time designated for showing a property to agents/brokers or to the general public.

Operating expenses. The costs a landlord, broker, or property owner incurs to run the business or maintain the building. This can vary widely.

Origination fee. The charge for originating a loan. This is usually paid at the closing.

Private Mortgage Insurance (PMI). This is offered by private carriers. See *mortgage insurance*.

Pre-approval. When a lender agrees to lend to a potential borrower in advance of actually securing the loan. The commitment remains as long as the borrower meets the qualification requirements at the actual time of purchase. Most buyers are not considered "serious" buyers without such pre-approval from a lender.

Principal. The loan borrowed from a lender, not including the interest or other fees.

Property manager. An individual who manages real estate for an owner. Duties may include collecting rent, overseeing repairs, and handling accounting and financial matters for the property.

Raw land. Unimproved land that remains in its natural state.

Real estate agent. A state-licensed individual who works for a licensed real estate broker and arranges and negotiates sales of property.

Real property. The full property, meaning land, rights, and anything attached to it.

Realtor®. A designation of a real estate agent from the National Association of Realtors (NAR).

Referral fee. A fee paid to someone who refers a client or customer that later buys a property.

Refinancing. A means of securing a lower interest rate, or other loan terms, by paying off one loan by obtaining another.

Seller's agent. An agent employed by the seller to do his/her best to sell the property. Seller's agents are responsible for listing the property, sharing information on potential buyers, and negotiating in the best interest of the seller.

Square feet. Commonly used form of measurement in real estate (in America) to define the size of a space. Length (in feet), multiplied by width (in feet) is the equation for calculating the square footage of a room.

Staging. A questionable, seldom used, practice of glamorizing the property before showing it.

Steering. The act of trying to direct (or steer) people away from a specific area and toward another area that is in line with the person's ethnic or cultural background or monetary status. Although hard to prove, steering is in violation of the Fair Housing Act.

Subagent. An agent who works as part of a deal that was initiated by another agent. One agent may list the property while another makes the sale.

Title insurance. Insurance that protects the lender in the event that any claims should arise that question the ownership of the property.

Title search. A check of public records to be sure that the seller is the recognized owner of the real estate and that there are no unsettled liens or other claims against the property.

Truth-in-lending. A federal law that obligates lenders to give full disclosure, in writing, of all fees, terms, and conditions associated with the initial loan period.

Zoning ordinance. Rules established by local government, which regulate and set guidelines for the use of property in a designated area.

Index

A

Appraisals, 89–90
Appraiser, 68–70
Aptitude and attitude, self-test for, 34–36
Assistance, 166
Assistant, hiring a, 167–168

B

Being best at what you do, 159
Benchmarks, using to keep your career on track, 168–169
Berman, Susan, Houlihan Lawrence real estate agent profile, 1–3
Big business, from local real estate agents to, 10–14
Books, list of, 197–198

Brand, Janet, Houlihan Lawrence associate broker profile, 137–138
Brokers, 61–62
commercial, 62–65
growth of, 9–10
Business plan, 175–180
Businesses, selling, 86–88
Buyers, representing, 83–86

C

Career
enhancement, 51–54, 60
is real estate for you?, 19–36
options in field, 59–75
Closing costs, 95–96
Commercial
brokers and agents, 62–65

real estate, going into, 153–155

Commissions, 74–75, 97–98

Competition, handling the, 112–113

Competitive analysis, 181–182

Conventions, 133–134

Courses, what to expect from real estate, 39–40

D

Deeds, titles, permits and other documents, 90–91

Designation, getting a, 157–158

Developer, 68

Disclosures and waivers, 116–117

Discrimination and fair housing laws, 115–116

Down payments, 92–94

E

Earning potential, 74–75

Education, training and background, 37–57

Errors and Omissions (E&O) insurance, 115

Evaluating your appropriate experience and skills, 138–139

Excelling and moving to the next level, 151–153

Existing firm, buying an established, 189–190

Expenses, start-up, 48–50

F

Fair housing laws, 10

Fairchild, Beverly, profile of agent

turned co-owner, 171–173

Falcone, Jo, profile of a Century 21 office manager, 59–60

Federal Housing Administration (FHA), creation of, 7–8

Ferri, Nancy, profile of Carrier and Associates agent, 101–103

Fiduciary responsibility, 114

Financial plan, 183–184

Firm, finding the one for you, 43–48

Fischer, David, profile of former intern, 123–125

Flexible hours, 29–30

Floor duty, 111

Franchises, 186–189
origins and growth of, 11–14
start-up costs of, 188

Future of your real estate market, 96–97

G

Galletta, John, profile of a new real estate agent, 19–20

Generating leads, 106–111

Getting ahead, 149–169

Getting hired, 137–148

Glossary, 203–212

H

History of business, 5–14

Homes not just houses, selling, 79–82

Homestead Act, 6–7

Housing boom of 1950s, 9–10

How do you like to spend your day?, 23–24

I

Industry today, the, 15–17
Internet sites, 78–80
Internships and part-time jobs, 125–129
Interview
acing the, 143–145
tips, 145–147
with real estate firms, 46–48

J

Job openings, finding, 142–143

K

Knowledge base, 22

L

Land broker and developer, 68
Leads, generating, 106–111
Learning from professionals, 129–133
Licensing exam, 40–42
sample questions, 54–57
Lippman, Sandra, profile of Prudential Centennial sales agent, 77– 79
Listings, studying, 140–141
Lott, James Taylor, profile of a real estate education, 37–38

M

Management team, 182–183
Market, factors affecting the, 14–15
Marketing, 161–162

Marketing plan/summary, 180–181
Mentors, 129–133
Mortgage broker, 72–73
Mortgages, 92–94
Multiple Listing Service (MLS), 116

N

National Association of Realtors (NAR) membership, 152–153
Neighborhood, know your, 88–89
Newsletters, 133–134
Niche, finding your, 141–142

O

Office
expenses, 106
manager, 59–60, 65–66
setting up your, 103–105
On-the-job training, 50–51
Open houses, 118–120
Opening your own
brokerage office, 156–157
office, 171–190
Operations plan, 182
Organizations and associations, list of, 191–196
Overview of field, 1–15

P

People person, are you a?, 24–25
Personality, "real estate," 33–36
Planning, 159–160
Player, becoming a, 155–156
Pre-interview skills, honing your, 139–140
Proactive, are you?, 30–31

Professional wisdom, 134–136
Property manager, 66–67

Q

Questions to ask a professional, 131

R

Recruiting, 184–186
RE/MAX, founding of, 12–13
Research, 120–122
   is it your thing?, 25–26
Researcher, 73–74
Resources, 191–202

S

Safety issues, 121–122
Salaries, 74–75
Self-managed career, 61
Sellers, representing, 80–83
Selling
   a property, a walk-through, 98–100
   businesses, not just office or retail space, 86–88
   successfully, 26–29
Singer Sewing Centers, 11
Skill and abilities, 31–33
Spending money to make money, 48–50
Staffing, 184–186
Staging, 82
Studying listings, 140–141
Suburbs, post-war expansion and emergence of, 8–9

Success in real estate, ten tips for, 166–167

T

Taxes, 91–92
Team players, 111–112
Time efficiency, 160–161
Timelines, using to keep your career on track, 168–169
Training
   and career enhancement, 51–54, 60
   education and background, 37–57
   on-the-job, 50–51
   ongoing, 43

U

Urban planner, 70–72

V

Virtual tours, 117–118

W

Walk-through the process of selling a property, 98–100
Warkala, Jean, profile of rookie of the year, 149–151
Web sites
   list of, 198–202
   your, 162–165
Work environment and your responsibilities, 101–122